LAUGHTER IN HEAVEN

UNDERSTANDING THE PARABLES OF JESUS

EARL F. PALMER

REGENT COLLEGE PUBLISHING
Vancouver, British Columbia

This edition published 2004 by Regent College Publishing
5800 University Boulevard, Vancouver, BC V6T 2E4 Canada
www.regentpublishing.com

Views expressed in works published by Regent College Publishing are
those of the author and do not necessarily represent the official position
of Regent College <www.regent-college.edu>.

National Library of Canada Cataloguing in Publication Data

Palmer, Earl F.
    Laughter in heaven : understanding the parables of Jesus / Earl F.
Palmer.

First ed. published: Waco, TX : Word Books, c1987.
Includes bibliographical references.

ISBN 1-57383-289-8

    1. Jesus Christ—Parables. I. Title.

BT375.2.P35 2004   226.8'06   C2003-907208-8

For our grandchildren and their parents

Anne and Greg Welsh—
Sarah, age 7; Emily, age 1½
Jon and Kara Diane Palmer—
Andrew, age 4; Tommy, age 2
Elizabeth and Eric Jacobsen—
Katherine, age 6; Peter, age 4; Emma, age 2

Seattle Preface

Jesus the Storyteller has always won both my heart and my mind. This is because the parables of Jesus invite us to welcome his love and faithfulness into our lives at every level of our awareness: parables that Jesus told engage our minds, they stir emotion and they assure our hearts.

I am grateful to Regent College, to Rob Clements and to Bill Reimer, who wanted to see this book again in print.

As a pastor here at University Presbyterian Church in Seattle, I preach and teach from the parables to my congregation in the context of 2004 and these stories of Jesus continue to challenge and disrupt in a good way just as they comfort all who hear them. The parables of Jesus never wear out.

My family is larger now, in 2004, than it was in 1986 when I first wrote this study. Our three children have families of their own and we have grandchildren who now are beginning their own journeys with the Lord who told us about the Laughter in Heaven after his story about one hundred sheep and the one that was lost until the good shepherd found him. I welcome all families everywhere into this joyous and good world of the stories of Jesus.

Earl F. Palmer
Seattle, Washington

Contents

Preface

This book will take a close look at the parables of Jesus Christ in the New Testament, both within their own first-century setting and then as windows through which we are able to understand our own life in the twentieth century.

In the first chapter we examine Jesus as a teacher and note the direct connection of his teaching method to that of Old Testament speakers, writers, and poets. The earthy realism of the Old Testament books is matched by the ways in which Jesus spoke to people during his ministry. That realistic and concrete approach is his approach too. The New Testament Gospels preserve for us those dialogue scenes of Jesus as he speaks and argues with people, answers their inquiries, and anticipates questions.

The New Testament also records our Lord's use of imagery and illustration. The most unforgettable teaching form Jesus made use of during his ministry is the parable. And it is these marvelous short stories I want primarily to focus upon and examine in this book.

The book will begin with the parables of the king, in which Jesus teaches about himself. The main subject matter of all parables is really the storyteller, but certain of the parables can be especially described as self-disclosure parables. These include the celebration parables of Luke 15: the One Hundred Sheep and the One, the Ten Coins and the One, the Two Sons and the One called the Prodigal.

There are also parables that I have described as the discipleship parables; these teach about the freedom that makes discipleship and faith possible: the Parable of the Soils, in Matthew 13 (and also in Mark and Luke), and of the Two Sons, in Matthew 21.

A third collection or grouping are the stories Jesus told about accountability—the parables of the kingly reign of Christ. These include the Parable of the Talents in Luke 19, and of the Good Samaritan in Luke 10.

There are also the parables of mystery and of Messianic secret, parables of promise and wonder, such as the Parable of the Temple in John 2 and the strange, acted-out, living Parable of the Fig Tree in Mark 11.

In each part of this book my goal is to endeavor to understand the ways Jesus taught so that, first of all, we as disciples of his kingly reign in our own generation will better know and understand the Teacher himself. Our second goal is to understand for our own time and space the will and purpose for our lives that Jesus reveals in his parables. Our third goal is to see ourselves in the parables, to understand and discover who we are in a way that a parable is able to especially reveal. For me, the parables of Jesus have not only been theologically challenging; they have also been personally challenging. There is a whimsical playfulness about some of the stories that Jesus told, just as others are deeply etched with the pathos of human suffering and grief.

If some parables are humorous and if others are tragic, they all are provocative, they all are pastoral, they all are invitations in one form or another to a banquet that is hosted by the teller of the stories, Jesus Christ the Lord, Jesus Christ the Savior. Even those stories that make us feel uneasy nevertheless draw us toward the storyteller so that we may hear more and know the endings of the stories. There is good news in the parables for all who read them because in the parables this storyteller invites those who hear his stories to trust in his faithfulness and to come home, to return to the place where we really are freest and safest. The stories he told help us to enter in and join in the banquet he has prepared.

I want to thank many of the people who have helped me with this book, those who are inspirational and supportive friends to me in my life work as a pastor and writer. I think of staff colleagues and the congregation of First Presbyterian Church of Berkeley, of colleagues at New College, Berkeley, my secretary Bonnie Johnston and my typist Mary Phillips, who have aided me greatly. I am grateful for my family: Shirley, my life partner, Anne and Jon and Elizabeth, our children who have grown up in our family with many stories we have loved to tell and hear. My mother and father, Ward and Myrtle Palmer, and Shirley's mother, Frieda Michaelson, with their stories too, have been an encouraging and vital part of our growing up. But of all stories we have loved, these that we learned from Jesus have been the best.

Earl Palmer
Berkeley, California
1987

Part I

Parables of the King

1

The Teacher

Why did Jesus of Nazareth tell parables?

It was not the only way he taught; he dialogued with people who asked him questions (John 14); like other rabbis, he read Old Testament texts aloud and commented upon those texts (Luke 4); he spent time with disciples and taught by the example of what he did (Mark 2). Like the prophets in the Old Testament, he distilled major themes into brief epigrams and concise sentences (Matthew 5). But Jesus also told parables. What are parables?

The two Greek words used in the New Testament for parables or figures, *paroimia* and *parabolē*, are translations of the Hebrew word *mashal*. In the Old Testament, the *mashal* or proverb is a story or an analogy. We find these *mashal*s throughout the Old Testament, especially in the prophetic books, in the Psalms, and in the book of *mashal*s (Proverbs). "They who wait upon the Lord will mount up with wings like eagles" (Isa. 40:31). The righteous are "like a tree planted by streams of water" (Ps. 1:3). These two well-known textual examples from the Old Testament are parables that express a concept by means of an illustrative image.

There are also parables that are short stories; some are humorous and some are frightening. The book of Proverbs includes one that is both:

> My son, if sinners entice you,
>   do not consent.
> If they say, "Come with us, let us
>   lie in wait for blood,
>   let us wantonly ambush the innocent;
> Like Sheol let us swallow them alive
>   and whole, like those who go
>   down to the Pit;
> we shall find all precious goods,
>   we shall fill our houses with spoil;
> throw in your lot among us,
>   we will all have one purse"—
> my son, do not walk in the way with them,
>   hold back your foot from their paths;
> for their feet run to evil,
>   and they make haste to shed blood.
> For in vain is a net spread
>   in the sight of any bird;
> but these men lie in wait for their own blood,
>   they set an ambush for their own lives.
>   —*Prov. 1:10–18*

This parable is a short story about the temptations to do that which is evil, and it is a story richly textured with both realism and ironic humor. The robbers have been so clever in designing their trap for an unwary traveler, yet to their surprise they are caught by the very trap they set. At the same time, the story's truthful understanding of human nature makes the parable frightening because we who read it see ourselves somewhere in the parable, either as trap builders or unwary travelers.

Why Jesus Used Parables

Jesus told parables like these, and he told them for two reasons. He told parables in order to be understood and so that his words would be remembered by people of every culture, in each generation, and in every century. Parables are unforgettable!

Secondly, by his own statement to his disciples in Mark 4:10–12, Jesus also told parables to keep his secret and to preserve his own mystery. This means that the parables of Jesus Christ are hidden—and yet they can be universally understood. They have two effects at the same time; they baffle us because of their hiddenness and yet they are so clear that twenty centuries after their telling we change our lives on the basis of what we learn from them. The hiddenness means that the parables belong to the storyteller; their clarity means that they belong to us.

Every parable in its deepest theological and ethical significance is a parable about the storyteller King and his kingly reign. At the same moment, because of the marvelous psychological and spiritual accuracy of the stories, each one has a way of finding us where we live and work as individual human beings. They arrest us right in the middle of our day-to-day relationships as members of families, as friends, as people in interpersonal relationships. The parables ring true to those experiences and the feelings that go with them, and this is why we cannot get these remarkable stories of Jesus out of our minds.

It is my goal in this book to take a journey through

the parables of Jesus and to observe many of them one by one, and first of all within the historical setting of each. Certain themes persist in every one of the parables, the most important being the way in which each one points the reader to the Lord behind the story. They also give us a highly focused look at ourselves, from a special angle that we shall observe as unique and fascinating. The third ingredient present in each of these stories and illustrations is what might be described as the disclosure of the will of God for each person's life. We have called these "kingdom parables" because of this disclosive reality.

Parables are literary forms of unusual interest, and Jesus made use of them in different ways. Some are told and then carefully explained point by point (for example, the Parable of the Soils, Mark 4). Some are left without additional comment so that they stand like a single lamppost along a forest trail (for example, the Parable of the Prodigal Son). Others then become in the hands of the storyteller a starting point for dialogue with his first-century listeners: "Which of these three, do you think . . ." (for example, the Parable of the Good Samaritan). Some are told in direct response by Jesus to an issue or a point of controversy (such as Luke 15:1–2). A few end with a challenge that recognizes our freedom in hearing and deciding: "'He who has ears to hear, let him hear'" (Mk. 4:9). But what is most important for us is that each of the parables is a part of the teaching of Jesus. Each is a part of the holy canon and therefore is God's word to us.

Parables leave the hearer with a mixture of unforgettable impressions, but there also is the possibility of misunderstanding them. Both go together. We understand parables because they are visual; at the same time we are able to misunderstand them because the visual nature of a parable turns them loose in our minds. The thoughts they stir up in our minds may not correspond accurately with the thought in the mind of the original teacher. Any teacher who tells a story takes a risk with the person who hears that story, and the Bible is a book that takes many such risks. Jesus was willing to risk his truth to the literary form called *parable* because he was so sure of his truth, and therefore parables are theologically and philosophically important demonstrations of his self-assurance as a teacher.

One last question we must ask is this: What language did Jesus speak as he told his parables? This is not as simple a question as some New Testament interpreters have previously assumed. Jesus probably spoke his northern Galilean dialect of Aramaic when he was teaching in northern Galilee. However, when he was in Judea, where Greek was more widely understood and spoken than Northern Aramaic, Jesus probably spoke in the Greek tongue.

Greek was the universal language of the first-century Mediterranean world, and it is probable that Jesus spoke Greek when in the more cosmopolitan Judea. The multiple linguistic nature of first-century Palestine is indicated in several places in the New Testament accounts. The charges fastened to the cross by the Roman procurator Pontius Pilate are a theologically important witness to Christ; but this also offers an important historical clue to the languages of first-century Jerusalem: Pilate ordered the charges against Jesus to be written in three languages. When Paul spoke in Hebrew during his defense before the crowd in Jerusalem, that fact of language choice by Paul is especially noted by Luke (Acts 22:2). Luke thereby signals to us that Paul would have ordinarily spoken Greek in such a situation. That the Old Testament was translated into Greek in the version known as the Septuagint, and the New Testament Gospels were written in Greek, are further important evidences of the widespread importance of the Greek language. "In the period succeeding the conquests of

Alexander the Great, the religions of the Near East learned to speak Greek. . . . Judaism was one of them," said C. H. Dodd, in *The Bible and the Greeks*. In that landmark study, Dodd carefully shows the influence of the Greek language through the Septuagint upon Jewish thought. On the other hand, W. F. Albright, the archaeologist and linguist, proves the enduring, staying power of Hebrew thought and language form in spite of the widespread influence of the Greek language. "The sayings of the leading Jewish teachers of the intertestamental and New Testament periods were preserved with remarkable tenacity for centuries," says Albright (*Matthew*, Anchor Bible, p. clxvi). He gives special attention to Hebrew and Aramaic proper names and place names that are faithfully preserved through their later presentation in the New Testament Greek (see pp. clxvii and following).

Other scholars have shown how the New Testament writers were able to write successfully in Greek though another language was their mother tongue. For example, the Galilean disciple John wrote his Gospel in a simple, though accurate, Greek. But his Greek reveals a writer deeply influenced by his Hebraic background. "If John wrote in Greek he must have had Aramaic as his mother tongue," says A. M. Hunter, in *According to John*. The point is clear—John could write plainly and clearly in the first-century lingua franca, but he dreamed and sang songs in his childhood language of Aramaic. The same was true of his teacher, Jesus.

Probably, Jesus was able to speak Greek fluently, but his imagery and his parabolistic story themes originate from his own culture and background, which was Jewish. This Jewishness of Jesus comes through in his teaching, especially in these wonderful short stories we call parables.

Nevertheless, it is also true that the teaching of Jesus

is not simply an extension of Jewish world-view perspectives. The imagery is both Jewish and ecumenical. There is a wonderful independence of Jesus from the categories of his Jewish root system. "The listener is never obliged to look for premises which would give meaning to Jesus' teaching, or to recall the theory about doctrines and traditions which he would be supposed to know beforehand. For Jesus never talks . . . from any particular point of view."[1] This is the storyteller we now must hear.

---

1. Gunther Bornkamm, *Jesus of Nazareth* (New York: Harper and Row, 1960).

2

Laughter in Heaven

Three parables stand together and were told at one time by Jesus in response to an awkward and stressful situation. Luke the narrator tells his readers of the strain created by Jesus' openness to and friendship toward people who were clearly recognized as sinners because of their acts against the public good of the nation Israel (Lk. 15:1, 2). Tax collectors were Jewish citizens who took advantage of the Roman occupation of Palestine for their own financial gain. They aided the Roman authorities in the taxation of the occupied nation of Israel, and for that aid they received personal protection and financial reward from the Romans. But they were hated by their own people, and therefore those who associated with them in any personal, unofficial way would be criticized (see Luke 19:1–10).

Luke portrays the public anger toward Jesus because of these unsavory friends ("the Pharisees and the scribes murmured, saying, 'This man receives sinners and eats with them'"). Because of that public resentment Jesus decides to tell three short stories: "So he told them this parable" (v. 3). These three parables are told with no follow-up dialogue or questions to the hearers. Nor does Luke tell us anything of the response of the people. Jesus does make two key comments at the conclusion of the first two parables, about joy in heaven. Therefore we know what those in heaven think of the stories, but not those in Galilee.

How are we to understand these three unforgettable stories as told by Jesus? First, it is clear that the stories speak directly to the stress created by the presence of sinners at Jesus' dinner table. In these stories Jesus describes lostness, and it is lostness that most poignantly portrays the person who, in his or her own identity confusion and greed, has decided to aid the oppression of a foreign occupying power—over against his or her own fellow citizens. Jesus also tells of the experience of finding a lost sheep or coin or son, and of how dramatically exciting that fact of finding really is. Moreover, in all three parables the major point of each story is the description of the celebration that goes inevitably with the experience of finding. Jesus also makes a theological statement of considerable importance as he declares that in the great family of heaven there is profound joy at the news of one sinner who repents.

More than any of the other parables in the New Testament, these three show the thrilling freedom and authority of God. That authority personally comes into focus in the *finding*, the *restoration*, and the *celebration* which are repeated themes in each parable. God is the finder, and the restorer, and he creates the party when that which was lost is now safely home.

Let us examine the lostness as a theme in the three stories. These parables portray four kinds of lostness.

So he told them this parable: "What man of you, having a hundred sheep, if he has lost one of them, does not leave the ninety-nine in the wilderness, and go after the one which is lost, until he finds it? And when he has found it, he lays it on his shoulders, rejoicing. And when he comes home, he calls together his friends and his neighbors, saying to them, 'Rejoice with me, for I have found my sheep which was lost.' Just so, I tell you, there will be more joy in heaven over one sinner who repents than over ninety-nine righteous persons who need no repentance."

—*Luke 15:3–7*

The first story tells about one sheep that is lost from a large flock of sheep. The flock of one hundred sheep is essentially secured in that all but one are at a safe place. But that one is "lost." Jesus then asks his listeners: "Would not every one of you risk the safety of the ninety-nine by leaving them in the wilderness in order to find the one sheep that is lost?"

The irony of that rhetorical question is that most knowledgeable listeners would answer no. The sheep may, in fact, be lost because of a disorientation caused by illness; and a potentially contagious animal, if found, may endanger the healthy flock.

In every parable of Jesus there is a surprise at the core of the story. In this story it is the apparent recklessness of the shepherd who puts the whole flock at risk, and so large a number at that, in order to find one single sheep. We are surprised by the priorities of the shepherd who so highly values one lonely, wayward sheep. There is, therefore, in the parable an interplay between the risk of endangerment toward the one and the risk of endangerment toward the whole flock if it is left unattended in the wilderness while the shepherd searches for the one. This tension gives to the parable its dramatic intensity. The lostness of the sheep is the lostness of inner disorientation and of separation from the community of sheep.

> "Or what woman, having ten silver coins, if she loses one coin, does not light a lamp and sweep the house and seek diligently until she finds it? And when she has found it, she calls together her friends and neighbors, saying, 'Rejoice with me, for I have found the coin which I had lost.' Just so, I tell you, there is joy before the angels of God over one sinner who repents."
>
> *—Luke 15:8–10*

Here we have an absolute and static form of lostness in that there is no disorientation or willfulness on the part of the small coin. Its problem is that it is out of sight; it has been lost by the woman in her house: "she loses one coin. . . ." Through no fault of the coin it is isolated and ignored by the users of money in the house.

It is important that Jesus includes this portrayal of static lostness precisely because it does not apply to the real condition of human beings except in the most extreme cases. Our lostness is not static, nor is it absolute except in those tragic situations where no choosing on our part has played any part in the lostness we experience. This is a circumstance in which others have lost us to their own awareness. Fortunately in the story, Jesus tells how the housekeeper remembers that a coin has been lost, and she searches for it. The coin can do nothing but wait silently (the sheep can bleat, and the sons can decide). Therefore, this portrait of lostness is the most desperate of all and its presence in the three short stories is a mark of hope for those who feel such an aloneness.

And he said, "There was a man who had two sons; and the younger of them said to his father, 'Father, give me the share of property that falls to me.' And he divided his living between them. Not many days later, the younger son gathered all he had and took his journey into a far country, and there he squandered his property in loose living. And when he had spent everything, a great famine arose in that country, and he began to be in want. So he went and joined himself to one of the citizens of that country, who sent him into his fields to feed swine. And he would gladly have fed on the pods that the swine ate; and no one gave him anything. But when he came to himself he said, 'How many of my father's hired servants have bread enough and to spare, but I perish here with hunger! I will arise and go to my father, and I will say to him, "Father, I have sinned against heaven and before you; I am no longer worthy to be called your son; treat me as one of your hired servants."' And he arose and came to his father. But while he was yet at a distance, his father saw him and had compassion, and ran and embraced him and kissed him. And the son said to him, 'Father, I have sinned against heaven and before you; I am no longer worthy to be called your son.' But the father said to his servants, 'Bring quickly the best robe, and put it on him; and put a ring on his hand, and shoes on his feet; and bring the fatted calf and kill it, and let us eat and make merry, for this my son was dead, and is alive again; he was lost, and is found.' And they began to make merry.

"Now his elder son was in the field; and as he came and drew near to the house, he heard music and dancing. And he called one of the servants and asked what this meant. And he said to him, 'Your brother has come, and your father has killed the fatted calf, because he has received him safe and sound.' But he was angry and refused to go in. His father came out and entreated him, but he answered his father, 'Lo, these many years I have served you, and I never disobeyed your command; yet you never gave me a kid, that I might make merry with my friends. But when this son of yours came, who has devoured your living with harlots, you killed for him the fatted calf!' And he said to him, 'Son, you are always with me, and all that is mine is yours. It was fitting to make merry and be glad, for this your brother was dead, and is alive; he was lost, and is found.'"

—Luke 15:11—32

This short story is the most unforgettable of all Jesus' parables. Its superb forcefulness and tenderness are heightened by the way it follows the first two parables. The great storyteller has stirred up the imagination and questions of his listeners by the first two parables that tell essentially two stories of lostness and the surprise of finding, and set forth the extravagant celebration that follows that finding. We who have heard the first two parables are already impressed by the risks that the shepherd has taken and the extravagance of the woman in her celebration of the coin that has been found. We have also begun to focus on the meaning of lostness because Jesus has used that key word in each of the stories. Now in the third parable each theme is more expansive and interrelated, but the simplicity of the first two has prepared us for this story which is profoundly more complicated in the questions raised and in the surprises that await us.

The Lostness of Bad Choices

The parable of the father and his two sons tells of two distinct kinds of lostness which become the third and fourth forms of lostness. In this parable, though, Jesus does not make use of the word "lost" until the close of the story.

The first son experiences the lostness of his own bad choices by which he independently chooses to abandon his relationships with father and brother in order to go to a far country. This is the lostness of frustrated ambition, the selfish aloneness that disconnects from family and traditional roots so that the basic identity of the son is compromised. That psychological-social-spiritual lostness is made visible when the money has run out and the son is without friends. The circumstance of vanishing wealth only makes visible the lostness of this arrogant aloneness. The story could have been told differently; the lad could have become so wealthy materially that "no one gave him anything." And in his circumstance of luxury the emptiness of his identity would also be revealed for the lostness that it is.

The Lostness of Anger and Self-Righteousness

But this third parable is a parable about *two* sons and the father. Jesus preserves the "lostness" thread throughout the whole parable. There is a profound lostness in the older son too. He is geographically close to the place where his father lives; nevertheless, this son is also lost. His is the lostness of anger and self-righteousness that isolates him from the father's celebration, the laughter in heaven. His own poor choices produce a lonely bitterness that makes him unsure of his identity—"I never had a party"—just as the wild carelessness of the younger son had produced an unsureness about his identity—"make me a hired servant." Neither son is sure of who he is.

If lostness is the shadow theme of these three parables, what then is their principal theme? They are supremely parables about God himself, who is described as the shepherd, housewife, father; these are primarily parables about the character of the Father. What we

learn about that character is what makes the three stories most important for the New Testament message
and for our understanding of that good message today.
We have learned from Jesus Christ that God is the one
who finds, who restores, who celebrates, and who takes
the risks and pays the price for these three good things
to happen. These are parables about the freedom of
God to be and do as he chooses, whatever the risk or
the loss. They are parables of kingly surprise, and the
greatest of all surprises is that through these stories
Jesus teaches us a fact about heaven that we could not
have known by ourselves or through our own specula-
tions. Jesus tells us there is joyous laughter in heaven
because of one single sinner who repents and who discovers the finding love of God. We discover that we as
mere individual human beings are of such great importance to God.

Like all the parables of Jesus, these three also teach
us about ourselves, because we too are in the stories.

Lostness is a human experience as is ambition and the
frustration of unfulfilled hope. The anger of righteous
indignation is an anger we live with every day in those
situations where we feel cheated or betrayed by other
people. The loneliness of fear and isolation from celebration is a bitter human experience that is as much a
twentieth-century experience as a first-century one.

We learn about the dynamics of lostness in these stories. We discover not only God's freedom to act in our
favor, as the waiting father acted in restoring his sons,
but we also discover through the story line of the third
parable and in the use of the word "repent" after each
of the first two parables that Jesus has preserved our
freedom too. The younger son "came to himself" and
said "I will. . . ." The older son is also called upon by
the father to decide and respond to the father's sovereign love. The father "entreated him."

Let us now ask, what do these remarkable parables

mean for us today in terms of the century we know and of the lives we live here and now?

God Is Able to Find Us

The parables show us that God is able to find each of us, regardless of how complicated our lostness is. We need to know this fact about God or we are in danger of seeing our lostness as a static and permanent fact about ourselves. This is the problem of the coin buried under a pile of old papers. If I once institutionalize and make permanent my lostness I will have then lost hope. These are parables of hope because they portray the active and persistent housekeeper-God who looks until he finds. God is the premier finder of all time. We must not entrap ourselves in a dead-end street as the elder brother did, imagining that he was not lost but that he had fulfilled the will of the father perfectly. He met a searching father who challenged as he loved his eldest son, who challenged the angry separation he had made from his brother. The father will not accept that anger as a permanent status of things.

God is a shepherd who is not worried about the contagious illness of this wayward sheep, or about the perilous entrapments that have made the finding very hard. This shepherd searches the dangerous hill country for even this sheep that has been already abandoned by the rest of the flock.

Finally, there is the lostness in a younger son, now repentant, who creates his own religious solution to his father's problem. "'I am no longer worthy . . . treat me as one of your hired servants.'" This religious son needs to meet the finding father who hears the son repent, but interrupts the son's religious solution with his own better solution: "'Put a ring on his hand . . . this my son was dead, and is alive again; he was lost, and is found.'" In each case of lostness, our eyes are on ourselves and upon our own understanding of the crises of lostness. In each case there is a surprise of holy intervention by the Lord of the story, and that intervention is the good news these parables tell.

One final surprise is the feast; in the celebration we realize how much we are loved. That whimsical, celebrative laughter of heaven is the best surprise of all in these parables. It is not laughter at our expense, but the laughter of thankful enjoyment for the costly love of the waiting father who makes each son welcome by taking upon himself each one's lostness, disarming its anger and despair.

In the Hermitage Museum in Leningrad is one of the finest collections of art masterpieces in the world. Most impressive of all are the Rembrandts that have been brought together in that one museum. Rembrandt's last painting, found in his apartment at the time of his death in 1669, is there. Still unfinished, but totally compelling and powerful, this is his interpretation of the Parable of the Prodigal Son, entitled *Return of the Prodigal.* Rembrandt has shown the father with his hands upon the shoulders of his son who has come home. The face and hands of the father totally command the attention of all who experience this profound theological interpretation of Jesus' parable. The hands are not the clutching hands of oppression, but the generous hands of salvation and freedom. They are able to reach down to this son and to reach out to the severe, elder son as well. They are kingly hands—but rugged, suffering hands, too. This is a painting of the gospel of Jesus Christ, and I thought when I saw it in the vast Leningrad museum that it is a dangerous painting to have in any country because it calls into question all of our values and the oppressive handholds we place upon the people around us. The painting tells a dangerous story of the God of omnipotence who is Lord of all and who proves his omnipotence, not by terror but by his love.

3

Four Debtors

"Therefore the kingdom of heaven may be compared to a king who wished to settle accounts with his servants. When he began the reckoning, one was brought to him who owed him ten thousand talents; and as he could not pay, his lord ordered him to be sold, with his wife and children and all that he had, and payment to be made. So the servant fell on his knees, imploring him, 'Lord, have patience with me, and I will pay you everything.' And out of pity for him the lord of that servant released him and forgave him the debt. But that same servant, as he went out, came upon one of his fellow servants who owed him a hundred denarii; and seizing him by the throat he said, 'Pay what you owe.' So his fellow servant fell down and besought him, 'Have patience with me, and I will pay you.' He refused and went and put him in prison till he should pay the debt.

When his fellow servants saw what had taken place, they were greatly distressed, and they went and reported to their lord all that had taken place. Then his lord summoned him and said to him, 'You wicked servant! I forgave you all that debt because you besought me; and should not you have had mercy on your fellow servant, as I had mercy on you?' And in anger his lord delivered him to the jailers, till he should pay all his debt. So also my heavenly Father will do to every one of you, if you do not forgive your brother from your heart."
—Matt. 18:23–35

This parable is in a place in Matthew's Gospel where Jesus is teaching his disciples about the importance of reconciliation between people. Following that teaching, Peter asks a question about the limits of forgiveness: "'Lord, how often shall my brother sin against me, and I forgive him? As many as seven times?' Jesus said to him, 'I do not say to you seven times, but seventy times seven'" (Matt. 18:21, 22).

After this extreme answer by Jesus, he continues with a parable that is a story told simply and directly about two people needing forgiveness. They are in debt, and the difference between the two debtors is, first of all, the difference in the amount that each owes. In the story this difference is very substantial. The one owes the equivalent of fifteen years' wages, a hopelessly large debt. The second man owes the equivalent of one hundred days' wages, a large debt but not as impossibly large as the first man's obligation.

The second difference within this parable is of much greater importance for the telling of the story, and that is the contrast between the persons to whom each debtor is obligated. The first man, a desperate servant, owes his debt to a mighty king who has compassion upon him and who by surprise forgives his debt totally so that the man is released from all bondage in connection with the debt. (The Greek word for forgive, *aphiēmi*, means literally "to abandon," "to leave behind.") The second man is indebted to this newly forgiven fellow countryman. Both are servants of the same king, but this man's misfortune is that he does not owe his one hundred denarii to the king. Instead, he finds himself under the brutal demands of his fellow servant. Whereas the first debtor was set free by the generosity of the king, the second is severely punished for his inability by his countryman. In the story, each man has the same essential crisis of heavy debt, but the difference is in the one to whom the debts are owed.

But this parable does not end at this first level. It is a two-chapter story that develops in the second chapter into a judgment/accountability parable. The king is angered upon learning of the harsh punishment that his first servant demanded of his second servant. The king's punishment is swift and definite, and with that punishment the parable ends.

Jesus follows the parable with an explanation of God's will as revealed in this short story: We who are forgiven are required to forgive.

At this point, we realize that the money has nothing to do with the first servant's stature before his king. The king will not be impressed by this man's ability to present large amounts of money, to repay his debt. In his forgiveness of a fifteen-year indebtedness, the king has already shown that money is not as high a priority for him as the people who stand before him in need. The man is judged in the second part of the story by the king because he forgot what had happened to him through the grace of his master. That grace should have changed his own motivation and priorities; he had experienced grace and, therefore, he should be able to share the very same gift that he had himself received. Instead he suppresses that very grace that had meant life and freedom to him and his family, and it is for this and this alone that he is severely judged in the hour of accountability. This is a parable about the king's character.

The Warning of Love

There is a warning in this parable and it is the warning of love; it comes from the kindness of God's character. The warning is that those who receive the goodness of God must allow that goodness to have its full, liberating effect in their lives so that it may flow through one human life toward another. Jesus concludes his teaching on prayer in the Sermon on the Mount (Matthew 6) with the very same warning. "'If you do not forgive others who have sinned against you . . .'" (Matt. 6:15). I like Martin Luther's wise comment upon this warning. He observes that we as forgiven men or women prove that forgiveness is indeed in our lives when we are able to share it with another. "See, this is the twofold forgiveness; one internal in the heart, that clings alone to the Word of God; and one external, that breaks forth, and assures us that we have the internal one."

But what we must see in this parable is that though the story is negative and disappointing in the heartlessness of this one servant, there are two grand positives in it. First, the parable shows how wealthy and strong is forgiveness on the part of the king. Forgiveness is able to set prisoners free from apparently hopeless situations; this powerful gift of forgiveness is positive and joyous in its result in human lives. Nothing can take away the marvel of the forgiveness that is totally unearned on our part. It is a liberating event so complete that the first servant is able to make vital decisions. In this story he makes a faulty choice, but nevertheless, the freedom to make that choice is what forgiveness is all about. When we are forgiven by God we are restored to a place of freedom toward our future. This is an inevitable conclusion that we discover in this parable.

The parable's second grand positive is the very accountability that Jesus announces to us. We are accountable for grace, and that accountability is not an evil burden but a good one. We are given a post, an assignment of responsibility in every experience we have of the love of Jesus Christ, and that responsibility is to share the love we have received with those who need it. We cannot escape that responsibility and we do not want to evade its wonderful obligating implications. According to this parable, the ethical obligations placed within our lives are placed there by grace. We have an evangelical ethic that originates in the prior love of Jesus Christ toward us. "Beloved, let us love one another . . ." (1 John 4:7). We forgive because we are first forgiven, which means that we learn about how to forgive from the king himself, and the greatest debt we owe to that wealthy king is the imperative that we do not forget his forgiveness toward us.

Why We Remember God's Forgiveness

This parable prepares those of us who are able to really hear it to understand the mystery of the Lord's Supper in which we celebrate and remember Christ's costly gift of himself to us. The instruction to us is simple, but very important: "This do in remembrance of me." This parable teaches us that now we know something of the dynamic importance of that remembering. We remember so that we may share the same grace we have received with an indebted world.

At another time during his ministry, Jesus told another parable that has certain similarities about it which resonate with this strong story. That second parable was spoken at a dinner to which Jesus was an invited guest.

During the dinner an embarrassing interruption took place in which a "woman of the city" came and began to weep and wash the feet of Jesus with her tears. In that awkward moment the Pharisee who was host to Jesus thought to himself, "'If this man were a prophet, he would have known who and what sort of woman this is who is touching him, for she is a sinner'" (Lk. 7:39).

Jesus was aware of these feelings in the heart of his friend the Pharisee and for that reason we have another classic parable about owed debts and powerful forgiveness.

> And Jesus answering said to him, "Simon, I have something to say to you." And he answered, "What is it, Teacher?" "A certain creditor had two debtors; one owed five hundred denarii, and the other fifty. When they could not pay he forgave them both. Now which of them will love him more?" Simon answered, "The one, I suppose, to whom he forgave more." And he said to him, "You have judged rightly." Then turning toward the woman he said to Simon, "Do you see this woman? I entered your house, you gave me no water for my feet, but she has wet my feet with her tears and wiped them with her hair. You gave me no kiss, but from the time I came in she has not ceased to kiss my feet. You did not anoint my head with oil, but she has anointed my feet with ointment. Therefore I tell you, her sins, which are many, are forgiven, for she loved much; but he who is forgiven little, loves little." And he said to her, "Your sins are forgiven." Then those who were at table with him began to say among themselves, "Who is this, who even forgives sins?" And he said to the woman, "Your faith has saved you; go in peace."
>
> —*Luke 7:40–50*

The parable is a brief, one-scene vignette in which two debtors are forgiven because of the generosity of a creditor. They owed different amounts, but they were treated equally to the same forgiveness by the creditor who absorbed the obligation of each. Like the Matthew parable, this one is about forgiveness; but in this instance we who hear the story make a different discovery. We learn from this story that our experience of God's kingly grace toward us in forgiveness causes gratitude and love to flow from our hearts toward the one who has absorbed the heavy obligation we were unable to satisfy. The Pharisee saw the point immediately and answered Jesus' question in favor of the greater gratitude from the greater debtor.

Jesus has made a very simple point in this story and in the question that he posed to his host. He has shown once again, as in the Matthew parable, that God is the one who cares about the burdens of debt we owe and that he is the only one who is wealthy enough to rescue such people with such burdens.

He also shows that our love toward God is related to our concrete experience of forgiveness. This second discovery has far-reaching consequences in that three great virtues—love, gratitude, and forgiveness—were inseparably united for the Pharisee by his conversation with Jesus. He learned on that day that human love for God grows out of our discovery of God's acceptance and healing love. Those religious people who were endeavoring to establish their worship upon some other foundation, such as careful avoidance of evil or nationalistic zeal, were to learn of the true and durable source of all worship of God. Worship is gratitude to the Lord for his saving grace.

From these two parables about forgiveness we have a very significant uniting of ethics and worship, of gratitude to God and lived-out grace toward the neighbor, whether that neighbor is a servant who owes us money

or a "woman from the street" who is in the room unin-
vited and unwanted except by Christ.

The Good Burden of Both Parables

In both parables, there is an unmistakable accountability. That accountability is a burden, but a good one.

In both, the Lord at the center of each story judges by
the standard of grace and that is the wonderful good
news in these parables.

A final observation is this: Both parables are spiritu-
ally and psychologically healthy in their outlook; both
are expansive and contagious with exciting implications
which make them contemporary to us in the twentieth-
century settings where we live. We have debts we cannot pay, nor will we ever be able to pay, and the good
news is of the lowly king who identified with each of us
at the cross on Good Friday in our behalf to fully pay
every debt. But there are others who have debts as well
and many of them owe those debts to us. These parables
unite our lives with theirs because it is God's will that we
share his grace with them. This is all good news, and its
salty taste is that we now know that God will hold us
accountable to share the love we have experienced. If
the Pharisee is watching Jesus, Jesus is also watching the
Pharisee.

4

The Existence of God

"There was a rich man, who was clothed in purple
and fine linen and who feasted sumptuously every
day. And at his gate lay a poor man named Lazarus,
full of sores, who desired to be fed with what fell
from the rich man's table; moreover the dogs came
and licked his sores. The poor man died and was
carried by the angels to Abraham's bosom. The rich
man also died and was buried; and in Hades, being
in torment, he lifted up his eyes, and saw Abraham
far off and Lazarus in his bosom. And he called out,
'Father Abraham, have mercy upon me, and send
Lazarus to dip the end of his finger in water and
cool my tongue; for I am in anguish in this flame.'
But Abraham said, 'Son, remember that you in your
lifetime received your good things and Lazarus in
like manner evil things; but now he is comforted
here, and you are in anguish. And besides all this,

between us and you a great chasm has been fixed, in order that those who would pass from here to you may not be able, and none may cross from there to us.' And he said, 'Then I beg you, father, to send him to my father's house, for I have five brothers, so that he may warn them, lest they also come into this place of torment.' But Abraham said, 'They have Moses and the prophets; let them hear them.' And he said, 'No, father Abraham; but if some one goes to them from the dead, they will repent.' He said to him, 'If they do not hear Moses and the prophets, neither will they be convinced if some one should rise from the dead.'"

—Luke 16:19–31

At its beginning, this parable gives signals to the reader that it is to be apparently a story about rich and poor folk and of the final justice of God in favor of the poor. But Jesus has a different goal in mind for this story, a goal that becomes clear at the close of the parable. It is a parable about a man who makes a major discovery of truth, but, unfortunately, his discovery is made too late. His life journey is completed. He finds himself in the place of death and at that moment he makes the harsh discovery that throughout his life he has badly chosen his journey. Unable himself to gain relief, he begs Abraham to warn his five brothers who are still living out their own life journeys and who are unaware of the torment ahead, a destiny that is certain because their life choices have been similar to his own. Abraham's reply to this troubled and unnamed man becomes the most important sentence in the parable—"'If they do not hear Moses and the prophets, neither will they be convinced if some one should rise from the dead.'"

With this parable, Jesus establishes some major theological ground rules for life. He makes it clear that the Law of the Old Testament (Moses) and the prophetic

messages of the Old Testament (prophets) faithfully prepare the way for every man or woman to discover God's
will for life. The ancient witnesses are faithful and true
and they still must be heard by men and women here and
now, and the way of righteousness to which they point
must be followed. There is enough truth in those faithful
witnesses for every man or woman. By this teaching Jesus
shows his own solidarity with the Jewish sacred Scriptures; he stands *with* the Old Testament and not against
it. He further implies that the good news of the kingdom
which he now brings in the new covenant is not strange
teaching that is contrary to Moses and the prophets of
Israel but is rather the fulfillment of their expectation.

This parable also teaches the necessity of human
choices about the Word of God in the Law and the
prophets. The five brothers must decide on the basis
of the witness that has been openly offered them in
their ordinary life journeys. The man who calls out to
Abraham asks for special and additional messengers
whom he hopes will force his brothers to pay attention
to the message of God's will, which he himself had evidently ignored throughout his lifetime. This request for
an overwhelming conversion of their senses is denied
him by Abraham. Jesus may be teaching that whatever
witness is to be given to humanity, it will neither con-
tradict Moses and the prophets nor overwhelm the
senses so that men and women are forced to acknowl-
edge the truth of God against their will.

The Trustworthy Character of God

But more than these theological themes is present in
this parable. Through the mouth of Abraham Jesus also
tells his listeners that even so great a sign as the resurrection from the dead will not be—for anyone who refuses
to hear the Law of Moses or the prophets—a sufficient
cause for faith. Faith must trust in the character of God

and his Word to us; faith that is won by signs of power is not the faith of relationship that knows the faithfulness of God; it is the submission of the will because of over-whelming power. This submission is by its nature a tem-porary acquiescence because it has been beaten and frightened by the show of force. Tomorrow this "faith" of acquiescence will require another miracle and a greater one in order to continue its submission to power. At the deepest level, the faith of acquiescence is a faith that is bought by the mixture of signs and fear, but "if men are converted because of fear they will later hate their con-version" (Martin Luther).

Jesus makes it clear to us that he has no intention of staging such conversions. His goal is the conversion that comes as we make the discovery of the faithful and good word of the Lord so that faith is in Jesus Christ and not any other source—whether of positive or frightful per-suasiveness. Jesus instead advocates a slower way to Christian conversion, maturity, and personal growth; it is the way that trusts in the word of God's character.

The implications of this parable for our understanding of the act of believing are very important. Belief is a relational, growing journey on our part as we discover and respond to God's nature revealed to us in the Law, the prophets, and supremely in the gospel. This means that faith takes time to grow. The high-speed-resolution experiences that have their origin in the show of power are not God's means for the building of faith in his peo-ple. The rich man thinks this will work with his brothers, but it will not.

I have seen for myself the truth of this parable that Jesus taught. It is accurate psychologically and spiritu-ally. People today trust in Christ because of the discov-ery of this person, the integrity and love of the man Jesus Christ. He wins their respect and finally they are persuaded to trust in his promises. All of this happens *before* the victory of Easter. That sign of genuine power over death is the authentication of a faithfulness already known and treasured. Resurrection is a vital authentication; but of itself or as a spectacle of sheer power it will not win a person to what God wants. The resurrection is awesome and powerfully persuasive to us because it is the resurrection of that man whom we have come to love and respect—the man who gave himself at Calvary in our behalf. Without Jesus, resurrection of itself would only prove power—but God is not concerned to prove only power. God has more important things to prove than power. It is the devil who seeks to impress and to tempt men and women with power, but God's plan is to assure men and women of his faithful love. That journey of assurance takes time; and it will take time for the five brothers to learn these proofs. Abraham cannot intimidate the five brothers with demonstrations of power because they would then have been tempted just as evil tempts.

No Shortcuts to Self-Discovery

We who read this parable sympathize with this unnamed man's request because we feel the sadness of his own personal distress and admire his concern for the other members of his family. This empathy that we feel toward the request that he makes of Abraham helps intensify our discovery of the parable's central focus. Regardless of the earnestness of our desire that certain people learn the truth that can save their lives and affect their destiny, nevertheless the fact still stands that there are no short-cut solutions to this discovery journey. God himself has decided that merely to override the human will in order to obtain compliance is against both his strategy and his character. (See C. S. Lewis's *The Screwtape Letters*, chapter 3, for a whimsical discussion of this truth.) The gospel of the fulfillment of the Law and the prophets in Jesus Christ will not compel our obedience by an absolute demonstration of power even though we may think this is what we want for ourselves or our skeptical relatives.

Faith is not compliance to the shock of present power; faith is trust in the word Jesus speaks and the work Jesus does.

When I was university pastor at the University Presbyterian Church in Seattle, I remember talking to a student who told me of the reasons for his agnosticism and of the many doubts he had about the reality of God. I asked him what he needed to know that would assure him. At that point he impulsively announced that he wanted something concrete to prove God's existence.

"Give me a specific instance. What would you take as concrete proof?" I asked.

At this he pointed to a little Japanese oak tree in the church courtyard. "I want lightning to split that tree at 12:01 exactly," he said. "Then I will believe in God's existence."

I told him I thought that that might be possible to arrange, but since it was then 11:58 A.M. I wondered if we could first schedule a trial run of the miracle. I suggested we imagine that the tree-splitting event had happened and that before we create such an agricultural crisis in the courtyard we begin the process of working through in our minds the meaning of the sign. One of the great things about the human mind is its ability to do just this sort of intellectual analysis. He thought my suggestion was logical. Therefore, we worked a while on a trial basis. I asked him, "The tree is now split at exactly 12:01. Tell me this. What has this concrete sign proved to you?"

We talked together about that question and in a few minutes we realized several things. The "miracle" had not proved anything of real importance. It had not *proved* the existence of God but only the existence of a spiritual and even perhaps demonic power a few inches above our physical, historical existence—a force that is able to play tricks on trees and people in Seattle. The incident had not proved anything about God's character and certainly not about his love or his respect for this young man. What we discovered was that the "tree miracle" would not prove anything that God wants to prove, or even of what we want to know. What God wants to prove has more importance and moral significance than can be demonstrated in such a sign.

Another real problem with my friend's sign was that it lacked sustaining permanence. He would need another sign tomorrow, and because of the human tendency toward sensory tolerance and addiction that sign would have to be larger and more destructive tomorrow. This is the real point that Jesus makes in his parable. Even the resurrection of someone from the dead will not produce faith. Lazarus, the brother of Martha and Mary, is raised from the dead in the presence of many witnesses, but that greatest miracle of Christ's compassion for people has decidedly mixed results. For some people, it produced wonder and the degree of amazement that helped to galvanize the crowd that hailed Christ on his entry into Jerusalem a few days after that event. (John's Gospel tells us that the raising of Lazarus was the main reason for the great crowd that met Jesus on Palm Sunday; see John 12:18.) But this miracle also became a stimulus to the coalition of religious opposition toward Jesus (John 12:9–11).

The only resurrection that will win faith is the resurrection of Jesus Christ, and that is because of who he is and what he said. We are won to faith because of the character of Jesus, and our faith is assured by the signs of his victory over sin, death, and the evil one (the devil). What God wants to prove to us will not happen with lightning bolts, but in the relationship experiences through which we come to know who he is. Jesus has taught us well and this parable helps to make it even clearer.

Part II
Parables of Discipleship

5

A Question of Time

The parables of Jesus are remarkable examples of his mastery as a storyteller. Two sets of literary contrasts are always present. First, each story is easy to remember; nevertheless there is a quality of hiddenness about each one so that the reader wonders about the choice of theme or characterization made by Jesus. This is the first contrast that marks every parable. Second, each parable has a simplicity about it as it presses the listener toward one or two simple, central points of the story; nevertheless every story also has an explosive quality about it causing the reader or listener to think of many possibilities. Each parable stirs up multiple images and brings more than one issue to our minds. Other contrasts and surprises act like hinges within the stories themselves, and these elements often become the most important clues to the meaning of Jesus' teaching within each parable.

These surprises at the heart of the parables also produce the most electrifying responses within each of us as
we read the parables and try to understand their meaning. For example, for us the experience of the surprises
in the Parable of the Prodigal Son, and his brother, create the explosive elements in that story which grip our
attention. As a result, we are sometimes bothered, sometimes baffled, sometimes encouraged, but always profoundly challenged by such a surprise as the father's
sovereign act toward the younger son or the elder son.

The simplicity of the parables also make them unforgettable. The very direct and obvious story Jesus told to
his Pharisee friend about the two debtors who were each
forgiven by a generous creditor is not a parable with sudden surprises hidden within it. The story is plain and
simple in its content and in its telling. What makes it so
powerful is the actual setting of the banquet and the
awkward presence of a forgiven person.

We now will consider a parable that directly relates to
the way we learn and hear these words of Jesus. Matthew,
Mark, and Luke's Gospels each record this Parable of the
Soils for us. They also narrate what Jesus said, after he
told the parable, how he explained the meaning of this
illustration and proverb about four kinds of soil.

And he told them many things in parables, saying:
"A sower went out to sow. And as he sowed, some
seeds fell along the path, and the birds came and
devoured them. Other seeds fell on rocky ground,
where they had not much soil, and immediately they
sprang up, since they had no depth of soil, but when
the sun rose they were scorched; and since they had
no root they withered away. Other seeds fell upon
thorns, and the thorns grew up and choked them.
Other seeds fell on good soil and brought forth
grain, some a hundredfold, some sixty, some thirty."
—Matt. 13:3–8

The interpreter of parables should look first for literary features in a given parable that provide the hinge of interpretation. In most cases the elements in the story that are repeated or which show marked contrast are the "hinges" on which the story turns. In this short story of a sower, the constant and unchanged element is the seed; it is the same for each place where it falls. The contrasting element is the earth upon which the farmer's seed is broadcast. Jesus defines the seed as the "'word of the kingdom'" (Matt. 13:19), "'the word'" (Matt. 4:14), or "'the word of God'" (Lk. 8:11). This is therefore not a parable about the sower and his powerful seed, because that element stays constant throughout. This should be described as the parable of the four soils because that is the variable feature upon which the story turns.

What do we learn therefore from this proverb? Regardless of the truthfulness of a fact or a word—and in this case we later learn that "the word" is the very word of God—even so great a word only becomes credible to a person when she or he is able somehow to hear it. This means that the truth of God's kingdom must wait for the right moment in any life before its liberating contents can become anyone's own truth and experience. We are therefore not surprised that Jesus would conclude this brief parable with the sentence, "'he who has ears to hear let him hear'" (Matt. 13:9). This parable teaches that for every idea or truth, there must be the right moment.

I remember clearly my first impressions as an incoming freshman at the University of California, Berkeley. During the orientation days at the time of registration, just before classes began, there were a number of festive events, such as the great dance at Hearst Gymnasium, the president's reception, and several seminars designed to orientate new students to life at the university. The seminars, which were optional, were presented by upperclassmen and were intended to help make our first months as beginning students more enjoyable and successful.

One seminar was titled—"What to do if you have academic difficulty." That seminar was very poorly attended; not a single one of us in my circle of friends took advantage of it. Why? The problem was strictly of timing, not content. During orientation we freshmen, at least I and my friends, saw ourselves as outstanding high school graduates. We had no intention of having academic difficulty! The seminar should have been offered about eight weeks later, and we would have been there! But at that moment, academic difficulty was not on our minds. The upperclassmen were answering questions we were not asking.

There is a basic principle here of learning and discovery which Jesus of Nazareth fully understood and explained in this agricultural story about the good seed and the four kinds of earth. *There is no discovery until the time is right.*

The vital question is, when is the right moment? The Parable of the Soils gives us some clues. Because Jesus' story is about a field and a farmer's seed we who hear it are able to listen to it at first without feeling threatened. As the parable unfolds, however, we the listeners become increasingly uncomfortable. And this comfort/discomfort level in our own feelings, as we hear the parable, becomes one of the hinges upon which the parable turns and makes its point. The story makes three things very clear.

The Moment Is Right When the Earth Is Uncluttered

At first, in any race between a ponderosa pine and a manzanita bush, the manzanita will win every time. This is because the manzanita is fast-growing and space-greedy so that a single pine sapling cannot possibly compete in the early weeks of the growth race. Every first-century farmer and every twentieth-century farmer/gardener knows about the early advantages of weeds and brush. The parabolic fact is that the word of the kingly reign of Jesus Christ is more like the ponderosa pine than the weeds and brush; it takes time for the word of God's kingdom to grow in a life. At first glance it seems no match for the weeds. But give it time to grow and give it the attention it needs in the early, critical days and the result is more substantial by far than a hillside covered by milkweed or manzanita.

How do you give a great truth like the gospel the time and space it needs?

According to Jesus there needs to be a clearing away of the clutter, just enough so that the plant you really want to grow has a chance to grow into the sun. Give a pine the soil—it does not need much ground space, just enough for light—and it will grow far up above the brush at its base and produce the lumber to build you a house. Since clutter is a very big problem in the life of the average person today this parable is quite contemporary.

One positive result that a crisis in our lives can have is the way in which weeds are revealed and exposed as weeds. When mid-term grades are low, the carefree student is sometimes shocked. And such a setback causes the student to reexamine priorities and to look more closely at what is actually growing in the field of his or her life.

Time itself is another aid in our task of examining what is growing in our lives. Weeds grow quickly at the beginning and fade away at the end of the growing season, whereas the pine stays small for a long while, but in the time of dryness it stands out among the rest. The gospel wears well over the long haul. That fact alone has given many people a second chance when they take a closer look at the values and life-style patterns that have begun to betray them. The "closer look" may lead people to rid their lives of some habits and attitudes and when such a clearing takes place, the soil becomes fruitful and suited to the substantial plants for which it was originally destined. Where clutter persists there is little hope for anything but random weeds, or the takeover by some earth-greedy brush that starves out even their best intentions. The person without priorities has invited weeds because that person has not thought about what should grow in the field. There is also the problem of the person with a secondary priority gone wild and overwhelming. The time is right when we recognize clutter for what it is and thorns for what they are. Only then are we ready to prepare some strategic ground for the plants that have their origin in the good seed of God's Word.

The Moment Is Right When the Soil Is Soft

Jesus tells about hard, footpath soil that is so hardened by the sun and the constant pounding of feet and animal hoofs that even though a seed may fall upon it, it is snatched away by a bird who is skilled in this very thing. The irony of hardened soil is that in any field the richest soil is the footpath soil where animals have walked and where plants have not grown successfully.

I believe that Jesus is here describing the tragedy of the hardened person, that man or woman who is permanently disappointed and cynical. Such persons will not allow any new life source within their lives. Because of a history of disappointment, they have built for themselves a shell of highly defended protection against the possibility of any more disappointment. I have learned one thing about cynical people and that is that they are usually, at heart, substantial folk who have been hurt and who now imagine that they will be hurt even more in the future unless they defend themselves against the possibility.

The solution is obvious—but not simple. Hardened

soil must be loosened just enough to allow the good seed
to start its journey of growth; the smallest crack in the
pavement will do because the life in the seed will overcome many obstacles of hardness. I have seen the marvelous California whitebark pine, that lives above the
timber line on Mt. Shasta, growing out of rocky ridges.
But the seed needs a crack in order to start.

Jesus of Nazareth is a master with hardened people;
we see the record of his skill in his encounter with
Nathanael (John 1) and with Nicodemus (John 3). A
story of the softening of a rocklike cynic in our century
is the story of the conversion of Malcolm Muggeridge. In
his book *Jesus Rediscovered* he tells of his own journey
toward Jesus Christ which reads like the transformation
of a rocky, alpine crag into the habitat for the majestic,
high-elevation, whitebark pine. For Muggeridge it took
a series of softening experiences that worked together in
his life to prepare him to risk just enough openness to
allow the possibility of God's love to enter in. When it
happened the journalist-cynic made discoveries that totally changed his life.

My own feeling is that hardened people, when they
finally open up to the love and trustworthiness of Jesus
Christ, make very good Christians. There must be a special sort of laughter in heaven at their entry into the
family.

The Moment Is Right When the Soil Is Deep

In this parable Jesus warns about thin soil that wel-
comes new truth but has only a superficial interest in the
process of growth. The problem with shallow soil is that
the real growing must take place beneath the ground
surface as much as above it. The roots of a plant need to
grow in proportion to the flowering part. In this thin-soil
illustration Jesus is describing a style of life that does not
work with the truth it discovers.

It is no secret that superficiality is a persistent problem in all human relationships and that for many moderns it has become a studied, state-of-the-art skill. Alvin Toffler describes the successful modern in his book *Future Shock* as one who is able to "relate and disrelate easily." This style of relationship enables a man or woman to cultivate relationships as long as they appear advantageous and then to transplant or throw them out when they appear disadvantageous. The only way in which this "skill" can work is that such a person must comfortably limit the depths of soil in which he or she permits root systems to grow.

Spiritually, this means a strong emphasis upon religious experiences, but not on discipleship and the hard work of learning. These folk attend to religion and ideology with enthusiastic initial interest, but they do not grow up all the way to maturity. Obsessed with a kind of spiritual and ideological wanderlust, they tinker too much with the plants and transplant them too much. The potential great tree is always that—a "potential" tree that is always dwarfed by the planter box in which it is rooted. The solution is depth, and depth comes with time and continuity.

This parable is about every man or woman who ever heard the words of Jesus and it is a freedom parable because it calls us to be the kind of soil we can choose to be—the soil that can produce the powerful tree with its one hundredfold potential, the sort of tree that is our gift from the Lord who is the sower.

6

To Finally Believe

"What do you think? A man had two sons; and he
went to the first and said, 'Son, go and work in the
vineyard today.' And he answered, 'I will not'; but
afterward he repented and went. And he went to
the second and said the same; and he answered, 'I
go, sir,' but did not go."[1]

—*Matt. 21:28–30*

Jesus told this story on the Monday of Holy Week to a
very nervous crowd. He followed up the brief parable
with a question: "'Which of the two did the will of his

---

1. Some translations have followed several ancient manuscripts in
reversing the order of brothers. For example, the New American
Standard Bible and the New English Bible record that the first son
said, "I will, sir" and the second son, "I will not." The significance
of the parable with each case remains the same. I have chosen the RSV
(and most other translations in their presentations of the text) because
the oldest manuscript, Codex Sinaiticus, sides with this rendering.

father?'" (v. 31). His listeners replied with the answer, "The first." Then Jesus addressed the people with salty words, stern words—but there is good news hidden in them.

> "Truly, I say to you, the tax collectors and the harlots go into the kingdom of God before you. For John came to you in the way of righteousness, and you did not believe him, but the tax collectors and the harlots believed him; and even when you saw it, you did not afterward repent and believe him."
>
> —*Matt. 21:31, 32*

How are we to understand this parable and statement? We begin by trying to understand the parable itself. The parable is brief but it is powerfully suggestive. In this story each son has a fault.

The first son too hastily opposes his father's will as if it were against him. He is defiant; he rejects the morning work suggestions of his father and stalks out of the house. But later on, his father's will makes sense to him and he does finally go to work in the vineyard. This son might be described as one who is a big problem at breakfast but a joy at supper.

The second son in this short story is quite different. He avoids conflict with his father, and says what he thinks his father wants to hear. His warm and cheerful agreement in the morning is an encouragement to the family still in shock from the rude hostility of the first son. "I go, sir." But as the afternoon wears on, it becomes clear that this second son has not intended to actually work. He could be described as a son who is a joy at breakfast but a big problem at supper. And this parable is, unfortunately for the cheerful lad, a supper parable, not a breakfast parable.

What is Jesus teaching in it?

First of all, this parable, as is true of all the parables of Jesus, shows that Jesus the storyteller really understands human personality. Just as the agricultural parables of Jesus are agriculturally accurate, so the interpersonal parables are psychologically accurate.

Jesus shows by means of this parable that he fully expects sharp and even negative reactions to the kingly claims of his Lordship upon our lives. This is a kingdom parable in which the main story line has to do with a claim that the father is making toward two sons. That claim is a strong claim and the stakes are very important. Therefore, the storyteller is not surprised that the first son resists that claim upon his life. In the way that he tells the story, Jesus shows his awareness of the intense and conflicting pressures that are focused upon that moment or series of moments in which a human being discovers the mighty claim of the Lord upon a life.

The parable also shows that Jesus fully expects the slippery response that comes from the second son. The teacher is neither surprised by the struggle of the rebel son nor by the temporary, staged agreement and apparent compliance of the second. Jesus' portrayal of the first son is very encouraging to all who have experienced the struggle of their will with the costly commands of the Law and the gospel. His portrayal of the evasive son may not be as encouraging, but it is equally important for us. Both portrayals keep the record straight.

The Comic and the Tragic

Two thematic threads are present in all good stories. And that is true here; there is one comic and the other tragic. The comic line is represented by the first son who, in spite of the strong objections of scorning fury, surprises the whole family when he finally settles down and goes to work in the vineyard. "What a surprise we all had from that boy. We never thought he would amount to anything!" There is rich comedy present in the turn of events.

The tragic line is represented by the second son, who misses out on everything important. His studied and polished agreeability at early morning cheat him of the chance to really meet his father. It would have been better had he spoken his mind and argued with his dad as the first son had done. A family argument at least causes people to get to know what each person is like and how each one thinks.

The second son's compliance was a device for avoidance, and it worked too well. The stormy first son came through his impetuous rebellion and then the changing of his mind. But the second son avoids all of that by a too-early and too-easy endorsement of the father's point of view. He has never really thought about the matter because he only said yes to get quickly away from the place where decisions are made. He misses out on the clarifying experience of repentance.

Finally, this son also misses out on the goal for his whole existence—the vineyard of God for which all of life is intended. He has failed to do the will of God. This is the final tragic element in the second son's story.

What is Jesus' principal teaching in this parable about two lads? Jesus decides to interpret only one theme from this story, and he imprints that one theme upon the parable by the question he asks: "Which of the two did the will of his father?" The one who did the will of the father is the one who believed the father.

This parable defines faith in a stormy and exciting way: as the mixture of hearing and doing the will of God. Therefore, we can correctly describe it as a parable about the meaning of faith—"believe" or "have faith".

Jesus speaks in the language of faith as he makes his challenge to the crowd. He scolds those apparently devout leaders who did not obey the "way of righteousness"

God had spoken to them of through his prophet John the Baptist: "and you did not *believe* him, but the tax collectors and the harlots *believed* him; and even when you saw it, you did not afterward repent and *believe* him" (Matt. 21:32 italics added). Notice how Jesus repeats "have faith" (in) or "believe" two times.

The parable makes a whimsical point in the story of the first son. It shows, in the words of C. S. Lewis, that "second thoughts are better than first thoughts." At first, this son is so sure that his father's will is wrong for him. But the longer he thinks about the matter, the more it makes sense to him, and finally, by the afternoon, it becomes clear to him that his father's will does indeed make good sense. The father's will wore well as the day progressed.

In the way Jesus describes it, faith actually benefits from the stormy, honest, vigorous examination of every possibility. Given time and the chance to think it over, the first son decided in favor of the father's will. C. S. Lewis captures this fact of the durability element in his discussion of the radical center of faith and its most basic source—the durability of Jesus Christ himself. Commenting on the "Grand Miracle" of the Incarnation, Lewis points out that this grand center lacks the "obvious attraction" of pessimism, optimism, pantheism, and materialism. Initially, each of these seems confirmed by multitudes of facts, but in time each encounters "insuperable obstacles." Conversely, the credibility of the Incarnation of Jesus Christ does not lie in its obviousness.

The doctrine of the Incarnation works into our minds quite differently. It digs beneath the surface, works through the rest of our knowledge by unexpected channels, harmonizes best with our deepest apprehensions and our "second thoughts," and in unison with these undermines our superficial opinions. It has little to say to the man who is still certain that everything is going to the dogs, . . . or that everything is electricity. Its hour comes when those wholesale creeds have begun to fail us.[2]

Jesus has shown us that it is better to finally believe what at first you cannot say than to say at first what you don't believe.

Faith in God is not meant to be a simple matter, and the parable of the two sons makes that clear. In a very few words, Jesus has set in motion some of the most complicated questions and possibilities about the real meaning of faith. From Jesus' story, we now know that human freedom in deciding is not taken lightly by the one who is the storyteller.

The Claim of God upon Our Lives

The parable also stands like a warning sign against the "Easy Street" speeches we are tempted to put in the place of the harder and longer lasting way of discipleship faith. This short story tells us about the struggle of deciding for ourselves about the claim of God's will upon our lives.

Let us examine the ingredients that come together in that decision of the two brothers. How can the claims of Jesus Christ become persuasive to a person in our century against such contemporary competitors as C. S. Lewis has portrayed for us: pantheism, materialism, optimism, or pessimism? Some people I meet are sure they have no problems that they cannot safely handle by themselves; they have no need for the Father's vineyard, nor does their world. They are *optimists* in a classical religious sense; self-contained and inner-oriented,

---

2. C. S. Lewis, *Miracles* (New York: Macmillan, 1960), p. 131.

they feel positive about the future of their own private kingdom.

When I was an undergraduate at the University of California, I remember standing one afternoon at the corner of Bancroft and College Avenue with a friend who lived in the same co-op as I. He had evidently been observing my journey of faith and my involvement in the dorm Bible study and the church college group with growing alarm. Standing next to a telephone pole, he was sternly warning me about what he considered the dangers of my slide into religious fanaticism.

He spoke with great urgency, "The trouble with Christians is that you depend too much on God when you should depend more on yourself; why do you need that crutch? Religious fanatics really make me furious!" And with that final statement, he hit his fist full force into the telephone pole to underscore his point. This was before the days of karate and kung fu hands of iron. He winced, but then he carried on as if everything were the same, because he was a philosophical optimist who needed nothing beyond his own resources.

I don't remember much more of the verbal part of that particular encounter, but his desperate emotional unraveling demonstrated to me the philosophical and psychological inadequacy of his classical, self-contained optimism. What I realized that afternoon was that it was my friend who was the fanatic, and I hoped for his sake that sooner or later his own myth of self-reliance would hurt as badly as his hand. Optimism as a religious-philosophical-psychological world view is a very dangerous fanaticism because it does not ask enough hard questions and is too quickly impressed by its own symbols of power.

Prince Andre in Leo Tolstoy's *War and Peace* is an idealistic optimist, and his powerful hero is Napoleon, just the kind of self-assured and successful man that

Andre himself wants to become. But a moment comes when everything changes for the young Russian soldier. It happens on the battlefield as Andre lies wounded and the hero of his life's journey comes into view. It is Napoleon making an inspection of the wounded prisoners of the battle.

Andre is surprised by how small Napoleon is as the emperor stands at the midpoint between the dead and dying prisoners and the vast dimensions of the sky. The larger concerns of Andre's dead comrades and of the possibility of his own death create a crisis for Andre. His Napoleonic world view, with its idealism of power, collapses at the very moment when he is so sure it would mean the most to him—the moment when he sees the great emperor in person.

My friend at the telephone pole may not have been an optimist at all. Perhaps he was at bottom a pessimist who was certain that in the end everything was badly and permanently injured, which is why he was preoccupied with crutches and why he put up with the physical pain of his hand impacting against the telephone pole. Pessimism has already decided that there is no help and, therefore, it accuses and denies ahead of time all affirmations of hope. But in the end, pessimism has nothing to offer but its warnings.

I have also wondered if his objection may have been, at least in part, a pantheist objection. Pantheism has focused its attention upon the inner divine consciousness of the human being, and therefore it is offended by the claim of the Christian gospel that God and he alone is the one who must speak for himself. Perhaps this is what bothered him about my weekly exposure to the Bible studies.

Materialism is also a strong possibility; like the pantheist, the materialist chooses an object for worship, that thing or energy which shall be for that person the center of focus. The very possibility that God is *extra nos* (outside ourselves) and hence able to make his own character known within human history, and on his own terms, is rejected because that is a very dangerous possibility both for the person who has already decided that divine reality is contained within the highly spiritual, inner consciousness of the human self, and for anyone trying to find meaning in the concrete opportunities and gifts of materialism. Faith in Jesus Christ wears well and survives the afternoons of our lives because of the eternal durability of its center, Jesus Christ himself.

7

The Good Shepherd

"Truly, truly, I say to you, he who does not enter the sheepfold by the door but climbs in by another way, that man is a thief and a robber; but he who enters by the door is the shepherd of the sheep. To him the gatekeeper opens; the sheep hear his voice, and he calls his own sheep by name and leads them out. When he has brought out all his own, he goes before them, and the sheep follow him, for they know his voice. A stranger they will not follow, but they will flee from him, for they do not know the voice of strangers." This figure Jesus used with them, but they did not understand what he was saying to them.

So Jesus again said to them, "Truly, truly, I say to you, I am the door of the sheep. All who came before me are thieves and robbers; but the sheep did not heed them. I am the door; if any one enters by me, he will be saved, and will go in and out and find pasture. The thief comes only to steal and kill and destroy; I came that they may have life, and have it abundantly. I am the good shepherd. The good shepherd lays down his life for the sheep. He who is a hireling and not a shepherd, whose own the sheep are not, sees the wolf coming and leaves the sheep and flees; and the wolf snatches them and scatters them. He flees because he is a hireling and cares nothing for the sheep. I am the good shepherd; I know my own and my own know me, as the Father knows me and I know the Father; and I lay down my life for the sheep. And I have other sheep that are not of this fold; I must bring them also, and they will heed my voice. So there shall be one flock, one shepherd. For this reason the Father loves me, because I lay down my life, that I may take it again. No one takes it from me, but I lay it down of my own accord. I have power to lay it down, and I have power to take it again; this charge I have received from my Father."

There was again a division among the Jews because of these words. Many of them said, "He has a demon, and he is mad; why listen to him?" Others said, "These are not the sayings of one who has a demon. Can a demon open the eyes of the blind?"

It was the feast of the Dedication at Jerusalem; it was winter, and Jesus was walking in the temple, in the portico of Solomon. So the Jews gathered round him and said to him, "How long will you keep us in suspense? If you are the Christ, tell us plainly." Jesus answered them, "I told you, and you do not believe. The works that I do in my Father's name, they bear witness to me; but you do not believe, because you do not belong to my sheep. My sheep hear my voice, and I know them, and they follow me; and I give them eternal life and they shall never

perish, and no one shall snatch them out of my hand. My Father, who has given them to me, is greater than all, and no one is able to snatch them out of the Father's hand. I and the Father are one."
—*John 10:1–30*

Chapter 10 of John's Gospel begins with the Hebrew words *Amen, amen.* These words are not typically used by Jesus at the beginning of a discourse but rather within discourses. (See 1:51; 3:3, 5; 5:24, 25; 6:26, 32, 53; 8:34, 58; 13:16, 20, 38; 14:12.) Therefore, we interpret chapter 10 as the continuation of the temple incident recorded in chapter 9.

The chapter begins with a brief proverb in verses 1–5. The Greek word used in verse 6—"figure" in the RSV—to describe the imagery Jesus creates of the shepherd and the sheep is the word *paroimia.* In the Septuagint, the early Greek translation of the Old Testament, this word and the word *parabolē* are both used interchangeably to translate the Hebrew word *mashal.*

The same word will be used in John 16:25: "'I shall no longer speak to you in figures. . . .'" Parables and figurative speech are used in John, but not so much in the short-story sense, as in the parables of Matthew, Mark, and Luke. But John's figures have the same overall purpose, that is, to teach by means of an analogy or illustration. A figure is presented by Jesus which the listener is able to understand by relating its meaning to his or her own experience. As we have observed throughout our study of the parables thus far, Jesus spoke and taught from a point of view that was earthy and concrete. Therefore, Jesus usually avoided the highly precise and oratorical tradition of the Greeks. He made use rather of simple analogy, allegory, and short stories as well as the didactic kind of teaching seen in its dialogue form in John's Gospel and in its distilled, epigrammatic form in Matthew, Mark, and Luke. In this tenth chapter, several of these forms of teaching converge in a single passage.

The proverb that Jesus tells in verses 1–4 draws several themes together as only a parable is able to do. Note two main ingredients. First, the parable begins with the image of a sheepfold; it has one door; the gatekeeper allows in the true shepherd; the sheep know the shepherd and the shepherd calls the sheep by name; the shepherd leads them and the sheep follow him.

Then, the parable introduces the negative possibility—the stranger whom the sheep will not follow because they do not recognize his voice. John tells us at this point that those who heard the parable did not understand its meaning. Therefore, as with the Parable of the Wheat and the Weeds in Matthew 13, Jesus decides to explain this parable; he gives meaning to several parts of the story line and, in fact, enlarges the story in his retelling of it.

Jesus, the Door of the Sheep

Let us attempt to trace what becomes the theme development as Jesus draws out several parts of the parable for his listeners: "I am the door of the sheep." Jesus is the entrance through which every truth, every teacher, and every disciple must enter. (In small mountain sheepfolds, the shepherd would often become the very door by sleeping across the opening to the fold.)

All Others Are False

All of the themes and teachers that do not enter by this doorway are false. Jesus has, by his interpretation of his analogy, made himself the very criterion of truth. He is teaching that every theme out of the past or in the present receives its meaning in terms of its relationship to this one door that God has established. The Law of

Moses enters by this doorway. When our special use of the Law does not submit to its fulfillment in Jesus Christ as the goal of the Law and the gospel, then that special use of the Law is false. This is what in fact happened in the case of the adulterous woman brought to Jesus in chapter 8, where the special use of the Law by Jesus' tempters distorts the true intention of God's Law. In that case what appeared to be the crowd's concern for the Law is instead recognized by John in his narrative as the thievery of God's Law. The men who asked their questions about the Law and of Jesus' judgment concerning the woman caught as a sinner are described by John as thieves and bandits seeking, not the good of God's flock, but its destruction, and the destruction of the very door itself. "This they said to test [Jesus]" (John 8:6).

Jesus tests every prophet, teacher, and teaching in terms of its relationship with the door. Even such apparently reverent language as the Pharisees used in their caustic discussions with the young man born blind ("'Give God the praise; . . .'" 9:24) does not pass through the door and therefore it is false. Their goal was to discredit Jesus Christ, not realizing that he was the very glory of God in their presence. The criteria for the true prophet have been set forth. Every prophetic promise or warning must become obedient to its fulfillment and that fulfillment is this remarkable single door through which all themes of Old Testament expectation converge and are resolved.

Jesus tells us that the purpose of his coming is in order that the sheep may have life and have it abundantly. This abundance is a fulfillment word that shows that the ancient yearnings of Israel not only inevitably point to Jesus Christ, but in that convergence they are truly completed so that they achieve their full goal and intention. They "go in and out and find pasture." Every theme in our lives, whether ancient or contemporary, finds its greatest fulfillment as it is subject to its true center.

Jesus, the Good Shepherd

Jesus further develops his interpretation of the parable. He is not only the door; he is the shepherd too. "I am the *excellent* shepherd." The word *kalos,* translated "good" in the RSV, carries with it the sense of competent, excellent. Jesus is the shepherd who does not lose his sheep. We have witnessed this shepherd skill of Jesus in the opening chapters of John's Gospel. Jesus found Nathanael; he found the woman at the well; he found the young man born blind ("Jesus heard that they had cast him out, and having found him he said . . ."—9:35).

But Jesus intends even more in the simile of the shepherd. He tells about the sacrifice that this shepherd will make in behalf of the sheep. He is not like the hired worker who has less at stake and therefore takes fewer risks in the face of danger. Jesus is the shepherd who risks his very life for the sheep, a risk that costs the shepherd his life. Jesus is the shepherd who, by his own decision, lays down his life—not as a victim, because even in death his authority remains. In this context, Jesus predicts not only his death but also his victory over death. Because his Father has willed it, Jesus lays down his life and will "take it again." That sentence is the fullest and most open prophecy concerning his coming hour that we have heard to this point in the Gospel of John.

Who Are the Sheep?

Within the total context of this dialogue, it becomes clear that the sheep are the ones who hear the voice of the shepherd (v. 3). The sheep follow him (v. 4). They do not follow the false shepherds (v. 5). The very names of the sheep are known by the shepherd and they know him (v. 14).

I do not accept Bultmann's thesis that John's Gospel makes use of the word "know" here because of Gnostic influence. Jesus' teaching and storytelling in this parable with its allegorical treatment is dramatically and wholly Semitic. The emphasis on name and the knowing of names is an example of just that Semitic kind of thinking. There is also a wonderful universality in the emphasis on names; sheepherders have named their sheep for centuries.

Jesus adds to this portrayal a further description: "And I have other sheep, that are not of this fold; I must bring them also, and they will heed my voice. So there shall be one flock, one shepherd." This further universal note greatly expands the parable, clearly stating in the words of the analogy that which Jesus Christ has been doing in his action. He has welcomed into the shepherd's fold people from a wide cross section and sweep of background and nationality, and along the whole social-acceptance scale. What a list! From the distinguished Nicodemus to the beggar born blind, including the Samaritan woman and a royal official from Capernaum, tax collectors, and other lost sheep: It is clear that "whosoever will may come."

The important theological point is that Jesus is the shepherd who invites the sheep into the fold. The only other criterion that matters is the willingness of the sheep to hear, to follow, and to enter. In this parable of Christ's authority, just as in the other parables that Jesus tells, the freedom of the shepherd and the freedom of the sheep are both preserved. But the authority of the sheep to decide upon which other sheep are to be approved for entrance has been disallowed by the shepherd himself. If and when we as beloved sheep take that authority upon ourselves, we then become the shepherd, and in the terms of this parable it means that we have become false shepherds because we have chosen a different door of entry than Jesus Christ and him alone. We have created a door of our own design. He is the only door. Therefore, racial tests for entry or nationalistic, tribal tests are against the clear teaching of Jesus Christ in this crucial passage. The only test we know of is how we stand with Jesus Christ himself. This is the only criterion.

Jesus decidedly does not teach that there are many shepherds and many flocks all journeying by separate paths to a great and holy destination. He is clear—there are many sheep from many places that he will draw together into the flock that belongs to the one shepherd.

John tells us that these words trigger a sharp division among the people. Some are profoundly impressed by Jesus' words and deeds while others remain baffled by it all. Still others feel that Jesus is possessed by a demon and is mad—they intend to stop listening. It is interesting how often in human history the charge of insanity has been used to disqualify the dangerous teacher. Alexander Solzhenitzyn as well as many other Russian intellectuals had the experience of being sentenced by Soviet authorities to mental hospitals in the Soviet Union. It was because their thoughts were dangerous to the doctrines of the state that they were considered mentally unstable. We owe a debt to the writer John for his careful record of these objections to Jesus; nowhere in John's Gospel are the opponents of Jesus and their arguments ridiculed by John; they are always seriously considered. This feature is especially true in relation to the theological objections to Jesus and his claims. In this parable Jesus himself has preserved for us some of the most vital teaching about the tests of theological teaching. Doctrines must be tested by their relationship to the Shepherd himself. Jesus remains a difficult problem to solve for everyone around him when the fact of that criterion is made really clear. But it is that centered testing that sets us free from every lesser doctrinal captivity. We now have the central focused reference point from which every secondary teaching may be evaluated.

Evidently the second part of the chapter (10:22–42) occurs later in the autumn, toward December. John places that part of the dialogue during the time of the Feast of Dedication (Hanukkah). In continuing dialogue with people who are confused as to who the person Jesus really is, he gives one more additional insight into the sheepherder figure: "'I give them eternal life, . . . no one shall snatch them out of my hand.'" This shepherd is not only the true shepherd; he is the shepherd who does not lose his sheep.

8

The Foundation That Lasts

Jesus concludes the most famous sermon ever spoken with a brief, unforgettable parable. This parable is really two stories told side by side. (The Parable of the Prodigal Son is also such a parable with two stories told together, first the journey of a younger son and then the journey of an older son.) The key to the interpretation of a two-story parable is to look closely for the parts of the narrative that are identical in each story and those parts that are different.

"Every one then who hears these words of mine and does them will be like a wise man who built his house upon the rock; and the rain fell, and the floods came, and the winds blew and beat upon that house, but it did not fall, because it had been founded on the rock. And every one who hears these words of mine and does not do them will be

like a foolish man who built his house upon the
sand; and the rain fell, and the floods came, and the
winds blew and beat against that house, and it fell;
and great was the fall of it." And when Jesus fin-
ished these sayings, the crowds were astonished at
his teaching, for he taught them as one who had
authority, and not as their scribes.

—*Matt. 7:24–29*

In this parable, notice those elements that are identical. The central figure in each story is a *house builder.*
Jesus does not precisely define the parabolic significance of the house. It is described as the house a man
builds—"his house." A house is the place where we live,
where we raise our families, and express our architec-
tural vision. All human beings according to Jesus' parable are house builders; whether wise or foolish, it makes
no difference in the parable. We build places to live,
enclosed spaces that house who we are. A house therefore signifies our identity and represents our philosophy
of life, our goals, our dreams. Some houses have large
family rooms. Some have swimming pools. Some are
small. Some are large. They express who we are.

According to the parable Jesus tells, we cannot avoid
this house-building. Even nondecisions erect a house
for us that we must live with. The student who cannot
decide about the school musical tryouts has in reality
made a decision by that avoidance nondecision. As a
result, he or she has missed the tryout deadline and,
therefore, will be living throughout the spring semester
in a house that does not include practice, rehearsals,
cast parties, audience reaction, and the chance to be on
stage.

There is no such thing as a nondecision that suspends
the movement of time and history. Therefore, we must
live in the nondecision houses we build just as we live in
the decision houses we build. We are all house builders.

Jesus does not allow for the possibility of any variable on this point.

A second constant in the two stories has to do with the storm. Every house we build will face a storm. The sentence that tells of the rain, the floods, and the winds is identical in each account. By this exact repetition Jesus makes it clear to his listeners that he is not teaching a parable about how to build houses where there are no storms. This is a parable about foundations and not about weather avoidance. This is not a teaching about the search for a safe context or setting in which to grow a family or a philosophy of life, an ideal environment where the climate is supportive and nonthreatening. Jesus has made it clear that every house we build must be able to endure a climate that is less than ideal. We will note in another story, the Parable of the Wheat and the Weeds, that he makes the same point (Matt. 13:24–30). The wheat must grow alongside the weeds until the time of the harvest. The farm workers ask the owner if he plans to pull up the weeds, but he replies, "'No. . . . Let both grow together. . . .'" Their special request for ideal growing conditions is rejected in that parable.

As Jesus comes to the close of the Sermon on the Mount, he alerts each of us who hear his words that we must prepare the houses of our lives that we are building for wind, rain, and floods. We must prepare the child for the road, not the road for the child. There inevitably comes a testing of all of the houses we are building, and that testing is built into the whole plan; no favorites are excused from this inevitable testing of the value systems and philosophies and dreams in which we invest our lives.

The variable in the parable is the foundation upon which the houses are built. From that variable, we discover the principal theological and discipleship teaching of the parable. And as the parable is the summation of the sermon, this teaching becomes a convergent point for the great themes of the ministry and self-disclosure of Jesus Christ himself. The parable is about Jesus.

A Messianic Parable

This convergence of themes teaches us two major conclusions. First, the parable is fundamentally a Messianic parable about the all-sufficiency of Jesus Christ himself as the fulfillment of the human search for foundation. He is the adequate foundation: "'Every one then who hears these words of mine and does them will be like a wise man. . . .'" Jesus has made himself and his words that Rock, the "Amen" that we are to wisely trust and build upon. The crowd of people at the lakeside who heard the sermon did not miss this obvious, Messianic-fulfillment language: ". . . the crowds were astonished at his teaching, for he taught them as one who had authority. . . ."

Jesus has posed a profound question. If I do not choose to trust my life to his words and to his character which sustains those words, then what do I propose to build my life upon? Will the foundation that I choose be strong enough to support the house in the nighttime hurricane as well as in the tranquil summer evening? Jesus' parable has forced the question out into the open.

The Freedom Choices We Make

Secondly, this parable is also a story about faith and the freedom choices we make. It argues from effect to cause and makes the case that since everything in life is tested, we therefore need to choose wisely what it is we shall trust. The parable has a point of view that is affirmed by the Teacher. When we have trusted in the words of the Teacher and the Teacher himself, we have trusted in the One who is faithful.

The words of Jesus are called "rock," and such an image serves as the "Amen" to the Sermon. The Hebrew word *Amen* is linguistically related to "foundation" and always has to do in the Old Testament with the faithfulness of God and our human trust in his faithfulness. That faithfulness is now personified before our very eyes as the Teacher of this parable makes himself and his work the rock. Therefore, we may wisely build upon his words; we do well to respond to this person. Faith builds upon the foundation and into the foundation.

I live in earthquake country. And the church I serve in Berkeley, California, is next to the campus of the University of California which sits astride the Hayward Fault, which itself is connected to the gigantic San Andreas Fault that stretches from Mexico to Alaska and directly under the city of San Francisco.

Earthquake specialists have pointed up several important facts about home construction in earthquake terrain: A wood structure, provided that it is bolted to its foundation, is ideally suited for the stresses of horizontal land movement, which is the terror of an earthquake. Another discovery is that 3/4-inch plywood corner reinforcements that extend the side walls of a house to the foundation will also greatly strengthen a house against the earthquake forces of horizontal land movement. In recent quakes it has been found that the nonbolted home moves a few inches away from its foundation, and that this move most often causes the collapse of the structure. A safe house is that house which relates as much of the house as possible to its foundation. It not only rests upon a rock; it is built into the rock.

I have often thought of the Golden Gate Bridge in San Francisco as our region's boldest structure in that its great south pier rests directly upon the fault zone of the San Andreas Fault. That bridge is an amazing structure of both flexibility and strength. It is built to withstand ten-foot vertical movement and to sway some twenty-two feet at the center of its one-mile suspension span. The secret to its durability is its flexibility that enables this sway—but that is not all. By design, every part of the bridge—its concrete roadway, its steel railings, its cross beams—is inevitably related, from one welded joint to the other, through the vast cable system to two great towers and two great land anchor piers. The towers bear most of the weight, and they are deeply embedded into the rock foundation beneath the sea. In other words, the bridge is totally preoccupied with its foundation. This is its secret!

Flexibility and foundation. In the Christian life, it is the forgiveness of the gospel of our Savior that grants us our flexibility; and it is the true Lord of the gospel who is our foundation. There is no other.

The true significance and durability of this parable in the last analysis, therefore, depends upon the authority of the teacher. Jesus has not allowed us any other option. Jesus' parable shows his wise understanding of the human creature. We are incurable builders, and we continually build our houses by rivers. Jesus does not scold us for building; in fact, his parable endorses that instinct. But if we have reasons to build the houses we build, most of all we need a Rock upon which to build them.

Part III
Parables of the Kingly Reign

9

The Friends of the King

The Parable of the Laborers in the Vineyard is told by
Jesus during his ministry just prior to his entrance into
the city of Jerusalem on Palm Sunday. The setting of the
parable is a place near the Jordan River; Jesus tells this
story to explain his kingly reign to his disciples.

"For the kingdom of heaven is like a householder
who went out early in the morning to hire laborers
for his vineyard. After agreeing with the laborers
for a denarius a day, he sent them into his vineyard.
And going out about the third hour he saw others
standing idle in the market place; and to them he
said, 'You go into the vineyard too, and whatever is
right I will give you.' So they went. Going out again
about the sixth hour and the ninth hour he did the
same. And about the eleventh hour he went out and
found others standing; and he said to them, 'Why do

you stand here idle all day?' They said to him, 'Because no one has hired us.' He said to them, 'You go into the vineyard too.' And when evening came, the owner of the vineyard said to his steward, 'Call the laborers and pay them their wages, beginning with the last, up to the first.' And when those hired about the eleventh hour came, each of them received a denarius. Now when the first came, they thought they would receive more; but each of them also received a denarius. And on receiving it they grumbled at the householder, saying 'These last worked only one hour, and you have made them equal to us who have borne the burden of the day and the scorching heat.' But he replied to one of them, 'Friend, I am doing you no wrong; did you not agree with me for a denarius? Take what belongs to you, and go; I choose to give to this last as I give to you. Am I not allowed to do what I choose with what belongs to me? Or do you begrudge my generosity?' So the last will be first, and the first last."

—Matt. 20:1–16

The surprise element in this parable is especially challenging and unsettling to the listener because the actions of the householder in Jesus' story threaten a very basic value system. Wages, in ordinary terms, are thought of as a return for work, with the amount of wages being in proportion to the amount of work. Whether the economic system be feudal, capitalistic, or socialistic, the rule of proportionate reward for work is a generally accepted principle. And though there are arguments about what constitutes "work," nevertheless the proportionate rule is universal.

This rule has been expanded by folk sayings that extend beyond the work place too. "You get out of life what you put into life" is an epigram that expresses this principle.

The most ironic feature of the surprise element in Jesus' parable is that our Lord himself has made the same point in conversation with his disciples immediately prior to his telling of the parable, "'And every one who has left houses or brothers or sisters,'" he told them, "'. . . for my name's sake, will receive a hundredfold . . .'" (Matt. 19:29). The positioning of the parable is itself an important clue to its meaning.

What is the teaching significance of this odd parable that apparently rearranges ancient traditions about work and workers? And what about the fairness principle concerning their pay by an employer? How should we understand this parable today and what influence should it have upon our life and faith?

The King's Authority

This is supremely a kingdom parable about the amazing and far-reaching authority of the king. Secondly, it is a discipleship parable, too, and it shows some of the surprises that we must get used to in serving the Lord of this kingdom.

First note what the parable teaches us about the owner of the vineyard, because it is he who hires the workers. The early morning workers agree to a wage which the householder faithfully pays at the end of the day. The second, third, and fourth groups are hired at different times, but they work without having contracted for any specific amount in advance. Instead of a wage agreement, the lord of the vineyard promises to do "whatever is right."

It is when the time of paying wages comes that the great surprise breaks in upon the story, and that surprise becomes the clue to interpreting the parable.

Jesus would have us interpret this parable from the vantage point of those laborers who worked all day, I believe. He tells the story in such a way as to emphasize their hard work, their bearing the "scorching heat." The element of surprise in the story would not make sense apart from this recognition by Jesus of the diligence and sweat of these all-day workers.

Had the story omitted the fact of their strenuous labor, we might have concluded that they had failed to do their job, and that would be sufficient explanation of the waves of new workers who were pressed into service throughout the day. The way Jesus told the story, however, does not allow such a solution to the crisis that developed at pay time.

Another subtle point in this parable is found in the fact that for the all-day workers, the crisis happens at the time of payment and not before. The workers are satisfied until the event of divine decision happens; then their anger surfaces. And that anger is the direct result of disappointed expectations. These two subtle factors—the vantage point of the all-day laborers and the surprising timing of the lord's payment—have prepared us to understand the parable's two major teaching themes.

The parable is about the hiring and paying methods of Christ the householder, and from it we make some very important discoveries about the reign of Jesus Christ. We learn that the lord of the vineyard is *generous*. It is his generosity that creates the crisis in the first place, because in no way has he been faithless or corrupt in his dealings with any workers. He kept all agreements that he had made, but he now exceeds the expectations of those who watch the event of final payment, especially in the case of the eleventh-hour workers who are paid so lavishly.

What becomes clear in the parable is that the Lord is Lord, and he refuses to submit to the logic of the complaints even of the employees who have worked all day with him in the vineyard. His reply to them leads them toward a deeper understanding of his grace. "'Friend,

I am doing no wrong . . . do you begrudge my generosity?'" This sentence bears a strong similarity to the father's entreaty toward his elder son in the Parable of the Prodigal Son. In each case the father/householder preserves his own authority, without wavering, and at the same moment there is a kindly invitation toward the discovery of grace by those who are confused by grace.

The Disciple's Responsibility to Understand

This parable also teaches about discipleship and helps those who are disciples of Jesus Christ, or who wonder about discipleship, to know what the kingdom of God is like. The parable shows that the all-day workers may in fact misunderstand the goals and the ways of the lord of the vineyard. This misunderstanding of Christ's ways is rooted in a misunderstanding of Christ's character. We should have known that the Lord of our vineyard is a gracious invitor of those who have no work. It is our problem, not his, that our expectations about wage equity have been so radically surprised. If we had paid closer attention to the clues that were always present in the character of Jesus of Nazareth we would have expected such extravagant behavior and generosity.

This is a parable in which Jesus helps his listeners to be realistic about the gathering of workers that is to be called the church. (The vineyard, in the Old Testament, is a symbol of the nation of Israel as a people of God.) Because of the parable we should not be quite as shocked or disappointed when we discover that even though Christian laborers have been at work with the Lord of the vineyard and in his vineyard throughout the day, nevertheless, they sometimes misunderstand the goals and the strategy of God. This is why at all times the church needs continuous checks and balances upon the fellowship and its leaders. Are we who work in God's field really aware of God's generous will? That healthy, steady critique comes from the standard of Holy Scripture, which is the faithful witness to the will and character of Jesus Christ. In this way the very parable we are reading is a check and balance upon our discipleship.

The parable has a moderating and humbling effect upon the servants of the Lord, but not a demoralizing effect. The wonderful good news about the generosity of the Lord stands at the center of the story Jesus tells and that generosity, though a surprise in the way it is expressed, is still the unchallengeable good news and criterion of evaluation. The gospel is the proper lens through which we read the small print of the biblical chart.

One more important element is present in the story— a fact that is almost hidden in it. The all-day workers have enjoyed throughout the day one distinct advantage which they forgot at the close of the day when wages were handed out. That advantage was the fact that they knew that they were hired throughout the morning and afternoon. As hard as they were working, they did so with an assurance that a fair wage would be paid them at the close of the day. This was not true of the others, especially the eleventh-hour workers. All day, from morning until five o'clock, they had waited and worried about how they could possibly feed their families that evening. Unemployment is a much harder and more demoralizing weight to carry than work, because of boredom and worry. Jesus highlights this anxiety thread in his telling of the story "'Why do you stand here idle all day?' '. . . because no one has hired us.'" The all-day workers shifted their eyes away from seeing the joy of their own security and of their established relationship as laborers in the owner's vineyard; they have instead focused their attention toward the very narrow and small matter of wage equity. Their concentration upon the question of rewards and payment has caused them to forget the joy of their own employment and the privilege that has been theirs to have been a longer time in fellowship with such a generous owner and employer.

The parable is a finely tuned psychodrama that has a very healthy, if unsettling, influence upon our lives in this century as we try to figure out our own part in the story. Jesus has drawn us toward a new way of looking at the kingdom of God. Once we get accustomed to this new understanding of the kingly authority of Jesus Christ we realize that we are in for a lot of excitement, especially toward the late afternoon.

10

One Road at a Time

One of the most beloved parables of Jesus is the one that
he told in response to a hard question that he was asked.
Luke is the only Gospel writer to narrate for us this
unforgettable short story that Jesus told to that lawyer
with the question. The parable is told in the context of a
discussion about eternal life.

According to Luke the questions of the lawyer are first
spoken in an attempt to tempt Jesus. Nevertheless, Jesus
seriously relates to the lawyer and asks of him his understanding of the Law. Finally, the lawyer poses a technical
question that was very much on the mind of all Jewish
nationalists of the first century, for moderates like the
Pharisees as well as extremists such as the Essenes at
Qumran, as well as Jewish citizens at large.

At the time of the first century, Jewish nationalism was
a tightly argued issue. The Gentile presence represented
by neighboring cultures and the Roman occupation

forces, made the question a vital and tough question. The Dead Sea Scroll discoveries have highlighted the intensity of the Essenes' feelings. They lived at Qumran during the time of Jesus and John the Baptist. Note, for example, the following prayer for victory found in those pre-first-century documents: "Blessed be the God of Israel. . . . He has gathered those who were stumbling but has gathered the horde of the heathen for extermination without survival. . . . All wicked nations are come to an end and all their heroes have no standing."[1] It is a question about identity that the lawyer asks: "'Who is my neighbor?'"

This is a profoundly important ethical question, because if the answer can possibly be broadened beyond tribal or national boundaries then the code of the Law becomes a heavier burden than if the boundary is narrowly defined. We do not know what the lawyer wanted or hoped to hear from Jesus except that Luke tells us he was concerned to justify himself. What he heard must have been as great a surprise to him as it is to us who hear this short story of the wounded man near Jericho.

And behold, a lawyer stood up to put him to the test, saying, "Teacher, what shall I do to inherit eternal life?" He said to him, "What is written in the law? How do you read?" And he answered, "You shall love the Lord your God with all your heart, and with all your soul, and with all your strength, and with all your mind; and your neighbor as yourself." And he said to him, "You have answered right; do this, and you will live." But he, desiring to justify himself, said to Jesus, "And who is my neighbor?" Jesus replied, "A man was going down from Jerusalem to Jericho, and he fell among

---

1. See p. 299, *The Dead Sea Scriptures*, English translation by Theodore A. Gaster (New York: Doubleday, 1956).

robbers, who stripped him and beat him, and departed, leaving him half dead. Now by chance a priest was going down that road; and when he saw him he passed by on the other side. So likewise a Levite, when he came to the place and saw him, passed by on the other side. But a Samaritan, as he journeyed, came to where he was; and when he saw him, he had compassion, and went to him and bound up his wounds, pouring on oil and wine; then he set him on his own beast and brought him to an inn, and took care of him. And the next day he took out two denarii and gave them to the innkeeper, saying, 'Take care of him; and whatever more you spend, I will repay you when I come back.' Which of these three, do you think, proved neighbor to the man who fell among the robbers?" He said, "The one who showed mercy on him." And Jesus said to him, "Go and do likewise."

—Luke 10:25–37

In this story Jesus sketches in for his listeners very brief, descriptive narrations about four kinds of people who encounter an Everyman figure who is simply called "a man," "a certain man."

The Thieves

The first group are the thieves. These are marauders who brutally beat and rob a traveler in order to steal his possessions. They leave him "half dead" after they have taken from him what they want.

Jesus shows no interest at all in the reasons these robbers might have to explain their action. He is not a Marxist who cheers on every form of class struggle because such struggle stimulates the necessary revolution of the oppressed. Jesus is more radical than Karl Marx ever could have imagined, and that revolutionary radicalism of Jesus is manifested in his angularity and defiance of every conventional and revolutionary historical expectation.

Jesus is only interested in the most radical event of that terrible afternoon and that event is the brutal attack by a gang of men upon one simple human being who happened to cross their path that day on the road from Jerusalem to Jericho.

The Religious Establishment

The second kind of person in the story is also represented by two people grouped together—a priest and a Levite. Both the priest and the Levite are a part of the religious and ethical establishment; both are priests, though the Levite is a priest with more limited responsibilities. Both men know the importance of the Law and its human advocacy which very provision the lawyer has brought into focus with his technical question to Jesus concerning the correct definition of "neighbor."

If any people should know the answers to such questions it should be the members of the priestly corps of the temple. But neither of the two priests stops to investigate the crisis or to help the person in crisis. Jesus shows no interest in the reasoning of the two priests as they briefly confront this human tragedy. What gives special hitting force to the story is precisely this spareness of detail offered by the storyteller at this point. The effect upon the listener, and the reader, is all the more powerful because we then must fill in the details for these two empty-faced noncharacters in the story. Are they frightened? Are they preoccupied? Are they rushing because of their own tragic circumstances? Do they simply not care? Are they avoiding involvement because they feel inadequate? The story Jesus tells is a powerful story because he does not answer these questions for us. Nor does he give even the slightest clues as to their answers. We learn, in the parables of Jesus, that the task of story-telling requires that the storyteller answer only the questions that need answering. This skill is also necessary for all discipleship teaching so that the one who learns—the would-be disciple—will bring himself or herself into the story.

The Innkeeper

The innkeeper also appears in the story and this person helps the wounded victim of highway crime because he has been requested to help and paid to look after the man. He is at risk in his service in that he must trust the promise of the Samaritan and also take on the special responsibility of a victim of crime, badly injured at that.

The Samaritan

The fourth kind of person we and the injured victim meet in this story is the Samaritan. We who read this Parable of the Good Samaritan are struck by the way in which Jesus carefully underplays the extent of the ministry of this Samaritan. What he does in favor of the man made helpless by vicious attack is that he delays his journey long enough to help; he offers some first aid; he exposes himself to possible danger from the same robbers; and he incurs some financial obligation. But notice how restrained are these descriptions by Jesus of the help of the Samaritan. The Samaritan does not stop his journey and take the victim back to Jerusalem to his own home for semipermanent care. He does not do orthopedic or brain surgery upon the wounded man. He does not obligate himself for the rest of his life financially to this man. Jesus is too good a storyteller and too wholesome a teacher to overstate the help of the Samaritan.

The Samaritan feels *compassion*. This word, which is key to the story, is the Greek verb *splanchnizomai* from which is taken the Greek term for "entrails." In the New Testament it becomes the word for the profound, physical feeling of identification and love that one concrete self has to another concrete self. When a person feels from his or her very center of physical being a strong awareness of caring identification toward another human being, that caring is called "compassion." It is a physical and concrete word used to express a person's concern in a physical, concrete way.

How are we to interpret this parable?

Our Lord made the focus very practical and ethical with his lawyer-conversationalist. First, Jesus transformed the word *neighbor* from a noun into a verb and asked the lawyer the question, "Which man proved neighbor to the man who fell among thieves?"

When the lawyer answered this question Jesus then said to him simply and directly, "You do the same. . . ." This is therefore a parable about the will of God for human life and human relationships; it teaches that we are to prove neighbor to our companions of the road. We are not to be thugs who rob and destroy, regardless of the reasons we may announce to justify such robbery. This parable clearly shows that individual human life is too important to be trampled upon and exploited. Jesus has spoken unambiguously against the violence that harms by day or night.

He also judges the more subtle violence of avoidance, of which the priests were guilty. But the surprise of the parable is that it is not pessimistic and cynical, because in fact there is the Samaritan and there is the innkeeper who cause a new and dramatic possibility to happen.

This is a "change-your-world" parable, and as such it is very realistic and very definite and very small scale. Jesus has shown his listeners that *where* we are at a given moment in history is of vital importance and nothing must diminish or blur that importance. We are not everywhere, but we are somewhere. I am not in Calcutta; I am in Berkeley, and the world is changed when ordinary people who have discovered the strength and motivation of the storyteller of the parable act in concrete ways *where* they are today.

By its restraint in describing the help, this parable teaches that the world is changed when individual "samaritans" make use of the particular giftedness with which they have been entrusted at each decisive moment. We cannot be everywhere and we cannot do everything, but we must act on the basis of the giftedness that we have. In this story the Samaritan is not a brain surgeon traveling in his completely equipped Winnebego with emergency operative theater ready for immediate use, complete with nurses and assistant. That wrinkle in the story would really harm its dramatic forcefulness. In this parable Jesus is the realist from start to finish, as he is the realist throughout his whole ministry. The Samaritan does not have all talents, but he does have a few, and those few talents are just enough to make the difference between life and death because the man is "half dead." What more do we really want! Sometimes we who listen to this parable want too much in the story. And our arrogant demands for luxurious solutions make us incapable of rendering first aid with what we think is the meager giftedness we already have in our hands. We wait for the ambulance to arrive when we ourselves should be hard at work doing CPR right now. The plain fact in the story is that the Samaritan was clear-headed and wise in what he did. What if the Samaritan had been drunk or if his vision had been blurred by religious or political technicalities which caused him to hesitate in inaction or wasted action? Had this been the case—and it often is in real life—then the story would indeed turn toward the heavy irony of moral tragedy.

Jesus shows that there are limited risks and costs in any decisive action we take that lives out his will for human life. But the parable is not defeatist in spite of the bad and/or indifferent characters in it—the gangsters and the priests. This is a parable of victory over evil just as much as it is a parable about suffering, costliness, fear, and indifference. Therefore the parable has a celebrative aftertaste.

An Unwritten Coda

We who love stories can imagine that unwritten coda to the story about which the parable hints. That moment would have occurred a few days later at the inn. By now the man who was beaten is well. He has notified friends from Jerusalem who have come to the inn to celebrate his rescue and recovery with him at a great party. At the dinner he stands to make a few remarks in which he tells the amazing account of his harrowing trip and its moments of sheer terror during the attack. He tells of the hours of waiting for help. He remembers two priests who passed him by without stopping. Finally, he tells his friends about the Samaritan who befriended him just in the nick of time.

In this final scene imagine the different human emotions as several travelers arrive at the inn. Two religious leaders en route to Jerusalem enter the inn and they are startled by the impressive crowd of city visitors; they step into the banquet room to see the distinguished Jerusalem guests and there is a moment of recognition between the priests and the man who is speaking at the head table. This moment of recognition is the definition of unhappiness and grief of the worst kind, because there is nothing for them to say or do. That chance for the priests was lost once and for all earlier on the road and now there is only a very dry feeling in the mouth and an overwhelming blanket of profound regret for them. I can think of no more lonely definition of the judgment of moral cowardice and disobedience to the commands of God concerning the human obligations of one neighbor for the other. These two religious leaders missed the moment of compassion for whatever reasons, and now the reasons seem totally petty and meaningless. There is the emptiness of nothing to say.

Another unhappy moment would occur if three highwaymen were to enter the inn, one wearing the gold ring that guests quickly recognize as belonging to their friend.

But the parable of Jesus is silent about such visits; he does tell, however, of the Samaritan who told an innkeeper that he would return to the inn and pay whatever was due for an injured man he had brought in during the middle of a night. It is this moment that is the best of all. There is a lull between speeches, at which time a man enters the inn door, goes to the desk and begins to ask a question of the innkeeper. "Do you remember me? I stopped here a few days ago and brought in a stranger whom I found in pretty bad shape. How is he doing? And what do I owe you?" The innkeeper smiles but does not answer; instead, he sends a messenger into the next room. There is a sudden cascade of sound, and so many cheers the stranger might think a wedding feast must be under way. Then a door opens to the banquet room and he recognizes the face of a man he had only met once before. This is happiness—the happiness that the gospel makes happen, the happiness that takes place when Christ's love flows through one human life toward another life. We can see now that when Jesus Christ calls us to the way of righteousness and the way of compassion he is calling us to the way of fulfillment and happiness.

11

A Matter of Importance

The Parable of the Talents is recorded in two places in the New Testament, in Matthew 25:14–30 and in Luke 19:11–27. The Matthew text tells us that Jesus told this parable during Holy Week. Luke places the parable just prior to Holy Week. Each narrative is emphatic in its time placement; therefore, it seems logical to conclude that, as with other teachings of Jesus, this parable was told on two different occasions and with somewhat different story elements in each telling. For our study we will examine the Luke text.

As they heard these things, he proceeded to tell a parable, because he was near to Jerusalem, and because they supposed that the kingdom of God was to appear immediately. He said therefore, "A nobleman went into a far country to receive *a kingdom* and then return. Calling ten of his servants, he gave them ten pounds, and said to them, 'Trade with these till I come.' But his citizens hated him and sent an embassy after him, saying, 'We do not want this man to reign over us.' When he returned, having received *the kingdom,* he commanded these servants, to whom he had given the money, to be called to him, that he might know what they had gained by trading. The first came before him, saying, 'Lord, your pound has made ten pounds more.' And he said to him, 'Well done, good servant! Because you have been faithful in a very little, you shall have authority over ten cities.' And the second came, saying, 'Lord, your pound has made five pounds.' And he said to him, 'And you are to be over five cities.' Then another came saying, 'Lord, here is your pound, which I kept laid away in a napkin; for I was afraid of you, because you are a severe man; you take up what you did not lay down, and reap what you did not sow.' He said to him, 'I will condemn you out of your own mouth, you wicked servant! You knew that I was a severe man, taking up what I did not lay down and reaping what I did not sow? Why then did you not put my money into the bank, and at my coming I should have collected it with interest?' And he said to those who stood by, 'Take the pound from him, and give it to him who has the ten pounds.' (And they said to him, 'Lord, he has ten pounds!') I tell you, that to every one who has will more be given; but from him who has not, even what he has will be taken away. But as for these enemies of mine, who did not want me to reign over them, bring them here and slay them before me.'

—*Luke 19:11–27,* italics indicate author's translation

Several of the parables of Jesus can be described as the "Coming-of-the-King" parables and this is one of the most famous of those. The setting of this parable has to do with the disciples' expectations concerning the timetable of the reign of the Messiah. Against the backdrop of that expectation Jesus decides to tell the story of a nobleman who went to a far country to receive his kingdom. Before he leaves, this man entrusts a great amount of money to each of his servants. (Each receives a mina, which is the equivalent of three months' wages for a laborer.)

During his travels the nobleman in Jesus' story receives a message that his servants have rejected his authority over their lives ("We do not want this man to reign over us"). This one-line inclusion in the parable adds a fascinating theological thread to the whole passage. We have in the story a situation where the workers in the estate have rejected the nobleman. Nevertheless, in spite of this disapproval, the nobleman receives his kingdom and returns to his original estate with all of his original power and even more, from new kingdoms he has gained.

Jesus Is Lord

Jesus has made one theological point clear before his story has even started and that is the fact that we, by our actions of faith or rebellion, do not determine the Lordship and authority of the Messiah. He is who he is because of who he is—not because of our vote or endorsement. We do not create Christ's authority as we create the authority of the city mayor or the President of the United States. Our faith does not *make* Christ king nor does our rebellion cancel his kingship. Instead, our faith *trusts* in Christ as king.

When the lord of the estate returns he calls his stewards to give an accounting of their trading mandate that they had earlier received from him. In the story there are three employees who answer. The first and the second have made a profit from their trading with the mina they had received. Each of them hears the divine accolade, "'Well done, good servant!'" The first servant is told: "'Because you have been faithful in a very little you shall have authority over ten cities.'" The second hears: "'. . . over five cities.'"

The third servant returns the single pound with a resentful complaint about the unfair expectations of the nobleman: "'I was afraid of you, because you are a severe man; you take up what you did not lay down, and reap what you did not sow.'" Following this encounter with the landlord the third worker is judged by the lord of the estate for his fearful nonaction.

The surprise in this parable is twofold: First, the lord of the estate does not in any way defend his original intention or commission in the face of the hostile complaint of the third worker. The nobleman is not defensive as we would expect him to be from our own experiences in such disputes. He does not challenge the bitter statement of his worker "'You are a severe man. . . .'" The worker has twisted everything and yet his twisted logic goes unchallenged.

The owner had in fact sowed, and sowed generously— a mina is a lot of money by any economic standard. Many economic wizards have started out on Wall Street with a lot less than such a legacy. Nevertheless, the nobleman accepts the angry complaint of his steward and then judges him from the worker's own standpoint: "Since I am severe you should have worked all the harder. . . ." There is a subtle and whimsical irony in this part of the parable. Jesus makes it clear that whatever standard we use—fair or unfair, twisted or accurate—the owner of the estate will still call us into a place of accountability. This is because the inevitable and inescapable accountability is the very point of the parable. The king is coming and the king calls every steward into a moment of accounting.

The second surprise in the parable is that the servant is judged, not because of bad investments, but because he was afraid and made no investments at all. He did nothing wrong, such as thieving, but he did nothing right either. It is very interesting that this surprise in the parable was a disappointment to certain second-century writers who evidently felt that Jesus' point was not very convincing. In the second-century book *The Gospel of the Nazarene* we find this parable narrated; however, it is "enriched" for us as the second-century writer decided to improve Christ's parable by adding a key phrase to the description of the third worker. We are told his error was that he "squandered his money on harlots and flute players."

Here is a good example for us who study the Bible of the dangers of enrichment of our texts; we should beware of all attempts to "enrich" and bolster the biblical accounts with luxurious additions. *The Gospel of the Nazarene* totally misses the surprise in Jesus' parable. Jesus is not telling a story about the moral chaos of wild workers. He is telling about fearful and careful folk who are doing everything they can to minimize the danger of risks because they do not trust the lord of the estate enough to obey his bold instruction. That is the surprise in the story. We had expected the selfishness of crime and embezzlement; instead we found the selfishness of fear and distrust. The key point is that this worker was not "faithful."

The reward to the faithful is more responsibility than they had before, and the joy of hearing the "well done" from the lord of the kingdom.

A good football player works very, very hard in spring practice in order to win more than "well done" words of approval by his coach; the reward a football player wants to hear more than any other is that he will be on the starting team in the fall. Think of this apparent incongruity! A youth works very hard in practice so that he will be rewarded with the chance to work even harder in the fall on Saturday afternoons in Memorial Stadium. No one wants to hear a coach say, "Well, Palmer, you have been such a hard worker at our practice sessions that I am going to reward you with a little well-earned rest this weekend at game time. You deserve it, believe me! This way you can watch the student rooting section card stunts and the marching band and have time to yourself to enjoy the game without the terrible stresses that go on out on the field. Congratulations, young man, you have earned this rest!" What kind of speech is that? No football player wants to hear such a speech. Yet we are always telling ourselves that we have too much stress and that we need to get away from stress and intense responsibility. The fact is that instead of escape from stress we need to avoid the bad stress that comes from fear and inaction, and guilt that comes from a distrust of the faithfulness of God. We need relief from bad stress, not good stress. We need all of the good stress we can take. Of course, we need it one Saturday at a time.

The Lord of the Gift Is Coming

We who are disciples of Jesus Christ in the twentieth century ask what is the meaning of this parable for our lives. Two major theological and discipleship implications emerge from it. This is a parable about hope. There is an eschatological wind that blows through its story. The parable teaches that Jesus Christ is Lord, not only in the present but in the future as well. Though humanity throughout the human story has in arrogance sent embassies to challenge his reign, the fact is unchanged that Jesus Christ reigns. This Lord is coming to his estate and that is news of profound hope as well. It means that we who have the various minas of giftedness in our hands should invest that giftedness with enthusiasm and boldness, knowing that the Lord of the gift is coming. This confidence grows out of the fact that Christ stands at the end of one's life journey just as he stands at its middle and at its beginning; it is this hope that gives to us the boldness to carry on a ministry in this world where we live.

There is at this point a connection to the Good Samaritan parable. We are not on every road nor do we have every possible capability of giftedness. But we are on this particular road here and now with the real mina that God has entrusted into our hands. We are responsible for this mina in this place and at this time.

The mystery of this parable has to do with the future vision that Jesus has given us in a brief unfolding. In this unfolding he assures his disciples that there remain for them, in the future destiny, and there extend for them into God's future plan, the entrusted tasks and responsibilities they have experienced in this present existence. The young man or woman in national ski patrol who is faithful in his or her mandate will look forward in heaven to slopes and ski runs that will challenge and fulfill the grandest expectation. "Ten cities for ten pounds." The parable upgrades the importance of our present duty and responsibility while at the same time it inspires the durability of our future destiny. Now we can better understand Bonhoeffer's statement: "We live each day as if it were our last and each day as if there were a great future. . . ."

How Can His Gifts Be Invested Beneficially?

The second discipleship implication this parable demands is its insistence upon the freedom and therefore accountability of every human being in the estate. Sooner or later, each one must encounter the questions of the lord of that estate. In this parable the workers had to think through the investment they had made; and we also are to ask the question—How can God's gifts that he's entrusted to me be most thoughtfully and beneficially invested?

God expects us to give this serious consideration. The third steward is challenged by the nobleman: "You knew. . . ." Thinking things through and making decisions are vital mandates throughout the teachings of Jesus, and especially is this mandate clear in the parables of Jesus. The word for prayers of intercession in the Old Testament is the Hebrew word which means literally "to think through, decide." Our stewardship of prayer is to be that kind of thoughtful experience for a believer before God. This is the word that is used by the prophet Isaiah in his description of God's house—"'My house shall be called a house of prayer for all peoples.'" The parable requires of us that we keep our minds clear and focused in order to invest wisely the mina of giftedness God has granted to our deciding care.

This obvious accountability and freedom mandate in the Parable of the Talents brings into sharp focus two practical concerns. Keeping our minds alive and focused so that we may be wise stewards of our ministry in the world requires that we *work* in gathering the information needed, whether it is scientific data or spiritual truth. Bible study is necessary for discipleship decision-making just as scientific research is necessary for engineering decisions. In both kinds of information gathering I need the help and constructive influence of other disciples alongside of my life and journey.

The 1986 Chernobyl nuclear disaster was made all the more dangerous because of the secrecy policy within the U.S.S.R. which caused scientists there to deny and suppress news of the extent of the crisis precisely at the critical time when the scientific community worldwide would have been most helpful. In order for help to come, there needed to be a flow of information. The same principle is true in the spiritual-discipleship journey of a Christian man or woman. We need the help of other Christians and of the biblical witness in order to really understand the giftedness that has been entrusted to us and to know of some of the possibilities that are ours to decide.

Finally, the parable calls upon listeners to keep our minds *clear* so that when the moments of deciding come to us we are not confused and self-preoccupied as was the third steward so that he exaggerated his fears of the severity of the land owner. Today in our generation we are witnessing an assault upon the clarity of the human brain. We are in danger of becoming a drugged society so that our minds are confused and fogged with forgetfulness and fear just at the very time when we need clarity and realism.

I realize the grave dangers that alcohol and all other drugs pose because of their power to produce addiction in users, but I am even more worried about a greater danger—the fact that all drugs and alcohol produce confusion. It is the loss of the clear head and the clear heart that is the greater danger. We need clarity today and the reason I do not want drugs or alcohol to affect my mind is just this fact: I do not want to fog my brain; it is the only means I have for deciding, and all of my life is involved in decisions. I want a clear head on Christmas Eve and New Year's Eve, too. I want to be able to relate and laugh and love with a mind that is not blurred. I also want to invest the mina that God has given to me. I know he will ask what has happened to it.

A Shadow Parable

But Jesus has also taught another stewardship parable which is like a shadow parable to the Parable of the Talents. This one is about an unjust steward.

He also said to the disciples, "There was a rich man who had a steward, and charges were brought to him that this man was wasting his goods. And he called him and said to him, 'What is this that I hear about you? Turn in the account for your steward- ship, for you can no longer be steward.' And the steward said to himself, 'What shall I do, since my master is taking the stewardship away from me? I am not strong enough to dig, and I am ashamed to beg. I have decided what to do, so that people may receive me into their houses when I am put out of the stewardship.' So, summoning his master's debtors one by one, he said to the first, 'How much do you owe my master?' He said, 'A hundred mea- sures of oil.' And he said to him, 'Take your bill, and sit down quickly and write fifty.' Then he said to another, 'And how much do you owe?' He said, 'A hundred measures of wheat.' He said to him, 'take your bill, and write eighty.' The master com- mended the dishonest steward for his shrewdness; for the sons of this world are more shrewd in dealing with their own generation than the sons of light. And I tell you, make friends for yourselves by means of unrighteous mammon, so that when it fails they may receive you into the eternal habitations. He who is faithful in a very little is faithful also in much; and he who is dishonest in a very little is dis- honest also in much. If then you have not been faith- ful in the unrighteous mammon, who will entrust to you the true riches? And if you have not been faith- ful in that which is another's, who will give you that which is your own? No servant can serve two mas- ters; for either he will hate the one and love the other, or he will be devoted to the one and despise the other. You cannot serve God and mammon."

—Luke 16:1–13

This parable of the unjust steward has baffled most interpreters for very obvious reasons. It is one of the strangest of all of the parables of Jesus because Jesus has chosen such impossible elements to fashion the story line of the parable. The steward of a rich man faces charges because of his wasteful management of the owner's estate, and he is soon to lose his employment because of those charges; everything depends on the accounting which the owner now demands from him. At this point in the story, the wasteful manager recognizes his precarious position. Should he lose his job, he is too weak to work and too proud to beg. He therefore becomes the shrewd liquidator of the owner's loaned assets. He informs debtors of very good news for them: If they pay to the estate part of what they owe, he as manager of the estate will forgive their entire debt. While he is still the steward of the estate he has this authority and therefore he uses the authority he has, even though its future status is decidedly unclear and fragile.

As the storyteller, Jesus commends, through the words of the owner of the estate this mixture of wisdom and boldness in the steward who made use of the one opportunity he in fact had at his command, to provide his employer with some return on the assets which had been entrusted to his stewardship. The key element in the parable's story is that this steward had very little time on his side because of the impending audit, but he had in his hands an authority, even if that authority could only last for a few days. The point of the story is that this steward made bold and skillful use of the only power he had at his command. He did not collapse into inaction or run away from the inevitable audit. Instead, he cleverly made arrangements with debtors that were generous settlements for the debtors, but settlements to the disadvantage of the owner of the estate. For this reason, the steward is described by Jesus in the parable as "the dishonest steward." But the steward was shrewd in one key fact; he saw the authority that was his and he made use of that authority.

Jesus follows this remarkable parable with an explanation in which he makes it clear to his followers that he, as their teacher, is not encouraging his disciples to love money and to devise various clever and even dishonest ways to have monetary success or advantage. The final sentence in his explanation of the parable is unambiguous: "you cannot serve God and money." This makes it very clear that Jesus is not advocating an avaricious monetary boldness on the part of his followers, which would enable them to conquer corruption with even more skillful corruption.

What does Jesus intend for us as the readers of this parable to learn and do as a result of the story? Jesus here teaches his disciples to make the fullest use of the time and opportunity that have been granted to them. We are not to run away from the challenges we face; we are not to collapse into inaction. We are to be shrewd in the sound sense of the word; shrewdness means to be skillful in making full use of the authority that is ours to use.

Jesus has really made that point clear in the intensified hyperbole of the parable's theme. Disciples of Jesus Christ have more far-reaching authority than does this dishonest steward. We have an audit ahead of us, as did he; however, our audit is not an event to be dreaded because of the vast resources of our advocate and friend, Jesus Christ himself. We have much more power and resources at our disposal than did this steward with his handful of debtors. Jesus is calling out to his disciples to be bold in exercising the beneficial resources that are entrusted into their (and our) hands. It is very interesting and significant that the dishonest steward "blessed" the debtors with forgiven debts. We are also to bless those who have fallen into heavy debt, and the joy of this "shrewdness" is in our discovery that the owner's plan is to forgive their debts, not dishonestly or for partial payment, but freely and openly. This is one more marvelous surprise granted to us in this odd parable, a surprise that makes even this difficult parable a good teaching in our favor.

12

Prayer

Jesus told parables about our relationship with God, and therefore, it could be argued that each one of them is in some way a parable about prayer. In chapter 18 of Luke's Gospel we find two parables that are told together; the writer Luke describes them to his readers as parables about prayer and worship. He introduces the first with this sentence: "And Jesus told them a parable, to the effect that they ought always to pray and not lose heart."

This first parable is followed by a second one about two praying men, with this introduction by Luke: "He also told this parable to some who trusted in themselves that they were righteous and despised others." These two parables are told together by Jesus and they should be studied together.

And he told them a parable, to the effect that they ought always to pray and not lose heart. He

said, "In a certain city there was a judge who neither feared God nor regarded man; and there was a
widow in that city who kept coming to him and
saying, 'Vindicate me against my adversary.' For a
while he refused; but afterward he said to himself,
'Though I neither fear God nor regard man, yet
because this widow bothers me, I will vindicate her,
or she will wear me out by her continual coming.'"
   And the Lord said, "Hear what the unrighteous
judge says. And will not God vindicate his elect,
who cry to him day and night? Will he delay long
over them? I tell you, he will vindicate them speedily. Nevertheless, when the Son of man comes, will
he find faith on earth?"

—Luke 18:1–8

This story portrays a corrupt judge who has no fear
of God or concern about people; the effect that this
strange, unrighteous judge has upon the story is to
heighten the surprise ingredients in the plot, and what
an incredible plot we have in this parable! It features a
widow who, in spite of her cultural powerlessness, gets
her way with a conscienceless judge because he feels
threatened or at least bothered by her. As if she could
with her fists do any harm to the powerful judge! The
parable is humorous because of the incongruity of a
mere widow's being so successful with such an unlikely
official. Had he been a true and honest judge, an even-
handed administrator who sought to establish justice
toward all people, regardless of their social status, we
might expect him to seek to honor her request. But this
judge is a ruthless man who cares only for himself. Nevertheless, he honors the lonely widow's request.

"Prayer Should Be Brief, Frequent, and Intense"

Why is this so? It is because he does not want to be
bothered by her pestering persistence. Jesus interprets

his own story by telling his listeners it is the boldness of persistence before God that he now invites of us. God is not offended by our strong yearnings and the concerns we dare to bring to him. One of the important ingredients in prayer is this urgency that arises from the deepest part of our existence and speaks out clearly, openly, and persistently. Martin Luther, in his commentary on the prayer Jesus taught in the Sermon on the Mount, gave the following advice to those who pray: "Prayer should be brief, frequent, and intense."

This is unquestionably a parable about the need for intensity in prayer. The result of this teaching is that Jesus has made the door of access to his Father wider still than we had ever expected. If a corrupt judge acts rightly in the circumstance the story describes, what of a judge who is not only fair and equable but who also cares about our welfare before we even ask? The sheer contrast in the parable prepares the listener to come before this greatest of all judges, who is not embarrassed by any needs or scandalized by the urgency the petitioner feels. He understands.

Jesus concludes his commentary on the parable with a question: "'When the Son of man comes, will he find faith on earth?'" This question shows that Jesus advocates urgency as a major ingredient of our prayers to God.

Prayer is to be a work we do with our minds and our wills. We are to persist in prayer, though the authority belongs to the true judge who acts speedily, unlike the unrighteous judge. This parable establishes for us the fact that *the good judge desires our earnest prayer*. We need not hold back in the hesitating fear that we are troubling him. This is the good news that comes full circle to Luke's opening invitation that we "ought always to pray and not lose heart."

The second parable is totally different in its mood and psychological atmosphere. Whereas the first one teaches the importance of boldness before God in the personality characterization of a powerfully assertive widow, in the second, Jesus teaches the importance of modesty and reverent hesitancy.

> He also told this parable to some who trusted in themselves that they were righteous and despised others: "Two men went up into the temple to pray, one a Pharisee and the other a tax collector. The Pharisee stood and prayed thus with himself, 'God, I thank thee that I am not like other men, extortioners, unjust, adulterers, or even like this tax collector. I fast twice a week, I give tithes of all that I get.' But the tax collector, standing far off, would not even lift up his eyes to heaven, but beat his breast, saying, 'God, be merciful to me a sinner!' I tell you, this man went down to his house justified rather than the other; for every one who exalts himself will be humbled, but he who humbles himself will be exalted."
>
> *—Luke 18:9–14*

In the first parable, Jesus is concerned with those who feel powerless, like a widow, who in the Middle Eastern culture of the first century was the poignant symbol of powerlessness. He urges boldness. Now, in the second parable, he warns against the danger of too much boldness and the cultic sectarianism that accompanies those who are so persistent in their praying that reverence toward God erodes into arrogance and insistence. Demands are made upon God that are insolent and impudent; such people do not trust in the character of God but instead demand certain specific results. When both parables are taken together, the result is a healthy and balanced life of prayer, a balance that is both trustful and without hesitation.

The second story tells of two men who went up into the temple to pray. One is a Pharisee. The Pharisee movement in the first century was a highly respected lay movement. It had its roots in the Maccabean revolt against the Syrians in approximately 168 B.C. Following that revolt the group of laity who struggled alongside the Maccabee brothers became disillusioned with the corruption that followed the successes of the revolt; hence, they became separatists and were gradually welded into a formal movement. The word *Pharisee* originates literally from the word *separatists* in Hebrew. This movement was a major force in first-century Jewish religious and political life and it should be no surprise to us that these devout men would be the ones who continually confronted Jesus with questions. They cared deeply about the issues of nationalism, and the Messianic hope, and especially, the Law. The Pharisees were widely honored by the general public which makes Jesus' choice of a Pharisee as a central character in the parable of special interest to us as we interpret the story.

The tax collectors, also represented in this parable, were a hated group of people throughout Palestine during the first century. These were Jewish citizens who traded upon their knowledge of their neighbors in order to aid the Roman occupation authorities in oppressive taxation policies. For this political help, they were offered the protection of Roman authority and generous commissions from the monies they were able to discover. Tax collectors were resented as betrayers of their society, who sold out the widows and the weak in favor of the powerful and rich foreigners. They had forsaken their tradition as Jews in favor of the present power of Rome.

We who read this parable twenty centuries later must try to understand the atmosphere present among listeners as they heard this story. Jesus tells of the prayers of a highly respected lay leader in the religious social movement, one who really cares about justice and tradition and the coming kingdom of God. Over against this leader of the people, Jesus tells of a tax collector—an oppressor of people, who nevertheless decides to come into God's temple to pray. The parable focuses its attention upon the content of the two prayers and the body language of the two men at prayer.

The surprise of the parable is totally shocking to our expectations because we are told that the corrupt exploiter of the people was not only heard for his prayer, but that he "'went down to his house justified.'" The man most admired for his social ethics, who fasts twice a week in order to give food to the poor, who is committed to truth, and marriage, and financial integrity—he becomes the one in this surprising story who did not go down to his house justified.

How Does Prayer Go Bad?

This amazing surprise causes us to ask: Where did the Pharisee's prayer go bad? What was right about the prayer of the tax collector?

The prayer of the first man begins well, but it quickly deteriorates. He begins by giving thanks to God, a very good beginning and one that is well-founded in the tradition of the Psalms and the prophets. But the Pharisee makes two major mistakes that drag him down to his house unjustified.

First, he is thankful for too small a matter. He has noticed himself alongside of other people and his eye has especially caught sight of a tax collector. He is thankful to God for what is at best an appearance of the righteousness that he knows is in himself, which he suspects is a greater achievement than that of the tax collector. But in the large scale of things his perception is really quite trivial. It is like being proud that our rug in the Presbyterian church on Channing Way is superior to the rug at St. Mark's Episcopal Church at Bancroft. This preoccupation with comparisons has shifted the Pharisee's gratitude away from the loving character of God toward the relative comparison of the stature of various people. But what positive value is this comparison to the one to whom it is announced? Does God need our evaluation of tax collectors? Is God Almighty not able to do his own measuring? Here is a man, supposedly at prayer, who has perverted the meaning of one of the greatest parts of the prayer vocabulary—the vocabulary of gratitude.

He is grateful for a very small matter, the fact that he is not like other people. But is this a discovery of such great importance after all? It is only important as a preliminary to the second mistake of the Pharisee's prayer.

He misses the chance to *bring* himself to the Lord. Instead he *describes* himself to the Lord. The tragic element in the Pharisee's prayer is this missed moment. Here is a man who shows God what God can see for himself. He misses a wonderful moment in which he could have simply brought himself into the generous presence of the Lord.

Too much of what we think is prayer is really descriptive monologue, either of the optimistic kind that presents such a litany of achievement as we hear from this Pharisee, or of the pessimistic kind that tells God how much we are unjustly abandoned and alone, and which describes the gloomy details of hopelessness in careful detail. In the end each of these descriptions is not prayer for help because we have avoided the essential vulnerability that has brought us to the Lord. We do not dare to ask for help because that would signal a certain inevitable loss of some of our power. Therefore, we describe and point up facts we feel God should observe and take note of.

Prayer Asks the Lord for Help

The tax collector does only one thing. He fearfully and timidly asks the Lord for help. "'God be merciful to me a sinner.'" He asks for the Lord's love, not his applause.

He is too overcome with the reality of his own sin to be grateful at the beginning of his prayer, though he will have very much to be grateful for at the close of his petition, because he experiences the righteous character of God in his own life. He goes down to his home justified.

The ironic thread in this parable is that very question with its two answers: What is it that each man has to be thankful for after his time spent at the temple of the Lord? The one is grateful for his isolation from other people by virtue of his superior lifestyle—especially from the tax collector. He leaves the temple unchanged and even more isolated than when he entered because he has religiously reinforced his lonely isolation during his time of "prayer." The second man is grateful for salvation, the wholeness that comes from God's love.

The impact of Jesus' teaching in these two parables that he told together is profoundly important to our journey of faith in the twentieth century. Any man or woman who is attempting to put together a theology of prayer needs to hear these two parables so that the two great themes—boldness and humility—may be united in a practice of prayer that is both devout and impulsive. We are invited to blurt out our prayers to the Lord and at the same moment to trust ourselves to the authority of the One to whom we make our prayers. The most fundamental element in all prayer is this: In prayer we bring our whole selves to the Lord. Then we make the discoveries of the surprises of his grace and sovereignty.

Part IV

Parables of Promise and Mystery

13

Invitation to a Banquet

There are two banquet parables that appear in the
Gospels of Matthew and Luke. Are these two different
parables here or are they one and the same? This is a
question that has puzzled the interpreters of these two
different Gospel narratives, each of which describes a
great banquet. Matthew presents one narration of a banquet scene.

And again Jesus spoke to them in parables, saying,
"The kingdom of heaven may be compared to a king
who gave a marriage feast for his son, and sent his
servants to call those who were invited to the marriage feast; but they would not come. Again he sent
other servants, saying, 'Tell those who are invited,
Behold, I have made ready my dinner, my oxen and
my fat calves are killed, and everything is ready;
come to the marriage feast.' But they made light of

it and went off, one to his farm, another to his business, while the rest seized his servants, treated
them shamefully, and killed them. The king was
angry, and he sent his troops and destroyed those
murderers and burned their city. Then he said to his
servants, 'The wedding is ready, but those invited
were not worthy. Go therefore to the thoroughfares,
and invite to the marriage feast as many as you
find.' And those servants went out into the streets
and gathered all whom they found, both bad and
good; so the wedding hall was filled with guests.

"But when the king came in to look at the guests,
he saw there a man who had no wedding garment;
and he said to him, 'Friend, how did you get in here
without a wedding garment?' And he was speech-
less. Then the king said to his attendants, 'Bind him
hand and foot, and cast him into the outer darkness;
there men will weep and gnash their teeth.' For
many are called, but few are chosen."

—*Matt. 22:1–14*

Luke also narrates a banquet parable:

When one of those who sat at table with him heard
this, he said to him, "Blessed is he who shall eat
bread in the kingdom of God!" But he said to him,
"A man once gave a great banquet, and invited
many; and at the time for the banquet he sent his
servant to say to those who had been invited, 'Come;
for all is now ready.' But they all alike began to
make excuses. The first said to him, 'I have bought a
field, and I must go out and see it; I pray you, have
me excused.' And another said, 'I have bought five
yoke of oxen, and I go to examine them; I pray you,
have me excused.' And another said, 'I have married
a wife, and therefore I cannot come.' So the servant
came and reported this to his master. Then the
householder in anger said to his servant, 'Go out

quickly to the streets and lanes of the city, and bring
in the poor and maimed and blind and lame.' And
the servant said, 'Sir, what you commanded has
been done, and still there is room.' And the master
said to the servant, 'Go out to the highways and
hedges, and compel people to come in, that my
house may be filled. For I tell you, none of those
men who were invited shall taste my banquet.'"
                                    —*Luke 14:15–24*

Are these the same parables? A similar story also appears in the second-century *Gospel of Thomas.* Is it the
same story, repeated for a third time? Richard Trench,
the noted interpreter, said that the Lukan and Matthean
accounts are of two different stories. I agree with him.

In Matthew's Gospel, the parable comes after the entry of Jesus into Jerusalem on Palm Sunday. In Luke's
account, it appears prior to his triumphal entry. Jesus
told parables more than once, and he told them in different settings, with different elements in the story line.
What I believe we have in these two texts are two stories
taught by our Lord on two different occasions.

In both parables the theme that is constant is that the
lord of the feast is the one who invites guests to enter
into the privilege of the banquet. In the account in
Luke, the feast is called a "great banquet" and the parable contains two surprises: (1) many of the intended
guests do not come to the feast because of their excuses,
and (2) the anger of the lord of the banquet results in his
wider generosity—a generosity which he shares with
people whom we would never expect to find at the feast
of a great and important host.

The Surprises in the Parable

We are surprised at the ones who ultimately are invited, and with the highly unconventional way the great
host extended the invitation. They do not seem to be the

type of folk we would expect to find at such a celebration. And what is more surprising, other more prominent guests whom we had logically expected to find at the celebration are not present. Moreover, the lord of the banquet announces that due to the bad choices of those originally invited, they will not be permitted to eat at the banquet.

What does this celebration parable teach us? Jesus is guest at dinner in the home of a Pharisee. He challenges his host to invite to his own banquets the very people who are unable to repay him his hospitality— the poor and the physically impaired. Then he tells this searching parable of judgment and generosity. From his previous comments we already know of the ethical concerns Jesus intends to teach his disciples about hospitality. But what seems to prompt the parable is the statement by one of the guests, who exclaims: "'Blessed is he who shall eat bread in the kingdom of God.'" These Messianic words of praise look toward the profounder banquet of the kingdom, a far more important event or occasion than the dinner parties or celebrations that are shared with friends and relatives and even the dispossessed.

At this point, Jesus tells the parable. A great host invites guests to dinner, he says, but he grows angry when he finds that the invited guests are too preoccupied and their lives are too cluttered to accept his invitation. Each excuse is plausible, but nevertheless it is finally only an excuse that keeps potential dinner guests away from the celebration.

Fundamentally the parable tells of the determination of God to invite people into this great feast, into relationship with himself. Because of this clear teaching we should not be surprised to find people at the glorious banquet table of God's presence whom we are not expecting to see there. They are "precisely the people we have hitherto avoided" (C. S. Lewis). The sovereignty of

the lord of the banquet is the major theme of this parable. His kingly reign extends beyond; it is a generous and
broad invitation, even to the street people who would
hardly expect so great a banquet.

The stern words of judgment are a part of the reign of
the lord of this parable as well. Note how he says: "'I tell
you, none of those who were invited shall taste my banquet.'" The lord of the banquet has both the right to
invite and the right to judge who should come to his
feast; this parable makes that double theme a major
teaching theme. The good news is given an antiphonal
counter-theme of judgment toward those who have
made a bad use of their freedom.

Matthew's portrayal of the great marriage feast given
by a king in honor of his son is also a parable of invitation, but the story line is more complicated with the
element of treachery on the part of several invited
guests who murder servants of the king. As in the other
account, the king decides that those who were originally
invited are now not worthy of his invitation, so people
from the streets are urged to attend. We are told that
those who are both good and bad come to the wedding
feast.

A Baffling Postscript

This parable includes a postscript that is very baf-
fling. If there is a sense of surprise in the generosity of
the king, we are now shocked by the king's harsh rejec-
tion of one of these newly invited guests, who is not
properly dressed. So marked is its departure from what
precedes it that Joachim Jeremias has concluded that
this stern postscript is "a wholly independent parable,"
and that it belongs in a different time frame.

Jesus himself concludes this parable with the enigmatic sentence, "for many are called, but few are chosen." This final sentence raises many hard questions for

us, but one fact is clear. Jesus preserves the fact that God is the one who invites and that we must be ready for the wedding, regardless of the timing of our lives. This parable preserves the responsibility of God as the Grand Inviter, but it also preserves our obligation to be prepared for the celebration. The clothing is the symbol of that preparedness. We must be clothed aright.

As this parable is mysterious and hidden in its portrayal of God's sovereignty so also Jesus does not instruct us as to the significance of these wedding clothes. We are to find that out for ourselves. But the key teaching is clear—we must be ready for the gracious invitation. Jesus has spoken more directly in other discipleship parables about that readiness—in parables about lamps and those who prepare for the coming of the bridegroom—but here in both of these parables of promise we are assured that there is indeed a great banquet of celebrative fellowship given by the father host. To this feast a very wide company of folk are invited, and we should be ready and waiting for that invitation.

14

The Hidden Parables

The Passover of the Jews was at hand, and Jesus went up to Jerusalem. In the temple he found those who were selling oxen and sheep and pigeons, and the money-changers at their business. And making a whip of cords, he drove them all, with the sheep and oxen, out of the temple; and he poured out the coins of the money-changers and overturned their tables. And he told those who sold the pigeons, "Take these things away; you shall not make my Father's house a house of trade." His disciples remembered that it was written, "Zeal for thy house will consume me." The Jews then said to him, "What sign have you to show us for doing this?" Jesus answered them, "Destroy this temple, and in three days I will raise it up." The Jews then said, "It has taken forty-six years to build this temple, and will you raise it up in three days?" But he spoke of the temple of his body. When therefore he was raised from the dead, his disciples remembered that he had said this; and they believed the scripture and the word which Jesus had spoken.

—John 2:13–22

John tells us that the Passover is at hand. This is the first of three different Passovers during the ministry of Jesus that John's Gospel will note.

In the temple area, Jesus found the money-changers and those who sold sacrificial animals. They exchanged the Roman coins, which were unacceptable for temple offerings because of the image of Caesar, into half-shekel Tyrian coins which could then be used for the temple tax. Caiaphas, as high priest, had allowed them to set up their tables in the Court of the Gentiles and so these religious merchants had placed their business stalls inside the temple precincts. The sale of animals in the temple area was unprecedented and contrary to ordinary temple practice, for if animals were to get loose they might violate the sanctuary.

Research into the first-century period has pointed up that the presence of large numbers of these merchants of sacrificial animals and of the money-changers stemmed from a controversy between the Sanhedrin and the high priest.[1] Caiaphas let in one group of merchants in order to penalize merchants who had sided with the Sanhedrin against him. Therefore, there is reason to believe that rival groups of merchants, taking advantage of this feud, were in the temple area.

Jesus enters the temple precincts, and takes everyone by surprise, though it is a pleasant surprise for all except the merchants. He turns over the tables! Then as neatly piled coins are scattered across the pavement, he makes

1. See Raymond E. Brown, *The Gospel According to John*, 1–12, The Anchor Bible (New York: Doubleday, 1966), 1:119.

a whip of cords and forces the traders out of the temple, turning loose the sacrificial animals to drive them out of the courtyard.

What a startling act! But what is most surprising to the reader is that no one among the leaders, or the merchants, or the people makes any move to stop Jesus. The most obvious explanation of this lack of resistance is that the people approved of his act. Jesus' words may have stirred the memory of those present, calling to mind the Messianic prophecy of David. John tells us that the disciples remembered words from a psalm of David: "'Zeal for thy house will consume me'" (Ps. 69:9). The people respond, not by scolding his action, but by asking what sign he could show that gave him authority for his acts. This is the very question one would ask of a prophet, to ascertain his credibility.

"Destroy This Temple . . . I Will Raise It Up"

The most interesting thing to note is that, according to the text, Jesus is not rebuked or threatened for his decisive act. Instead, the act is accepted, perhaps even welcomed, by most of the people. They are perhaps weary of the chaos caused by the large numbers of tables and cages that have crowded in upon the temple since foreign idols were brought there by Antiochus IV in 167 B.C. Now the remarkable Galilean rabbi is purifying the temple of the home-grown idols of avarice and greed and exploitation. So the people ask for a sign and Jesus' reply is enigmatic and hidden as he gives them a spoken sign, a parable of total hiddenness: "'Destroy this temple, and in three days I will raise it up.'"

Those who hear his words try to understand them in their most obvious sense. They remind Jesus that forty-six years have already been spent in the rebuilding of the great temple. The temple at Jerusalem has played a very significant role throughout the history of Israel.

It had first been built by Solomon about 950 B.C. It was destroyed in 586 B.C. by the armies of the Neo-Babylonian Empire. Seventy years later it was rebuilt on a very modest scale by Zerubbabel. In 20/19 B.C., Herod the Great began a major rebuilding which was to result in a temple on a more magnificent scale than even that of Solomon's time. According to Josephus, the project will finally be completed in A.D. 63. This project, along with other impressive building ventures, gives us some idea of the tremendous wealth of the house of Herod and the importance of Jerusalem as a city.

Jesus has given a hidden sign to the people which is at once both incomprehensible and unforgettable. The people do not understand what he really means, yet they feel uncomfortable and anxious because of what he says. At the same moment Jesus has given a sign they will not forget. In fact, his words, twisted out of their original intent and shape, will be used against him in his trial (Mark 14:58). False witnesses will accuse him of saying he would destroy the temple. At the cross we have the record of those who mock Jesus: "'You who would destroy the temple and build it . . .'" (Mark 15:29, Matt. 27:40). Also, Luke records in Acts 6:14 that at the trial of Stephen his accusers claimed that Jesus said he would destroy the temple.

The sign Jesus gives at the temple touches on a raw nerve. This, I believe, accounts for the electrifying effect of his words. The temple is a vital and symbolic national place, and Jesus has dared to suggest its possible destruction. He has, by the spoken sign, taken the symbol of the nation's life into his hands.

A Shocking Sign

It is very important to note that in the text Jesus does not make any effort to correct the misunderstanding of his listeners. He is willing to allow the sign to stand as it is: He allows the ambiguity to persist. So the sign shocks the crowd who hear it. It is mysterious by any standard: How can this man possibly rebuild the temple in three days? If the sign is mysterious, it is at the same moment, authoritative. Most of all, the sign has an awesome and dangerous, apocalyptic feel about it. "'Destroy . . . I will rebuild . . . three days.'" Only later, after the sign is fulfilled by Christ himself at Easter, will it make sense to those who have heard these words. Then they will understand the sign of these days.

The disciples are no better off than anyone else concerning this strange parable of Jesus when it comes to understanding its meaning. For them as well as for the others it is totally mysterious and hidden. The sign takes its place among the secret Messianic sayings of Jesus: "Jesus did not trust himself to them" (John 2:24).

This becomes another instance in which Jesus is prepared to allow great signposts to stand along the path which apparently do not seem of any present help to the journeyers, except that Jesus himself is the one who speaks the sign.

There is a technical question we must still ask. How are we to reconcile the timing of this temple incident in John and the event described in the synoptic Gospels? The synoptic accounts place the cleansing of the temple after the Palm Sunday entry into Jerusalem, but John records this event near the beginning of Christ's ministry. Those interpreters who argue against John's positioning feel it improbable that such an affront against the temple would go unchallenged by the authorities. These arguments, by C. H. Dodd, C. K. Barrett, and others, are not so convincing to me. The evidence in the account demonstrates that what Jesus did was not rejected by the people, but welcomed. There is here, I believe, a parallel to John the Baptist who, though he had a stern and judgmental message, was nevertheless popular with the people. It is not at all improbable that Jesus' act in the temple was welcomed by many of the people at large, and perhaps even by members of the party of the Pharisees, which could help us understand the Nicodemus interview of the next chapter. Remember that Nicodemus comments upon the "signs" that Jesus does.

Some commentators favor John's placement in preference to that in the synoptic accounts (J. A. T. Robinson, for example). Another hypothesis (see B. F. Westcott, *The Gospel According to St. John*) is that Jesus on two occasions confronted the money-changers and salesmen in the temple, once at the beginning of his ministry and a second time after his triumphal entry into Jerusalem. This option is not improbable because it fits with what we know of the tenaciousness of human sinfulness. We should expect that not long after Jesus himself left the temple the tables would be set up again. This view makes the most sense to me.

The really important thing that happened at Jerusalem during this first visit is that, by what he did and said, Jesus planted a signpost in Jerusalem. That signpost is clear about one thing: the mysterious authority of Christ—"I will build up." But its deeper, richer meaning will remain hidden until his death and resurrection. It is something like the strange lamppost which the first visitors to Narnia find in the Winter Kingdom in C. S. Lewis's *The Lion, The Witch and the Wardrobe*. It is not until much later that the meaning of the lamppost becomes clear. Nevertheless, it plays a part in the story. It sheds a strange and real light and helps the journeyers to find their way too.

So it is with the signs of Jesus in the Gospel records; so it is with the parables of Jesus. Each signpost along the way has meaning within itself and at the same moment points beyond itself. In no instance is one of the signs perfectly clear or complete; in each case it is helpful yet disturbing, illuminating and confusing all at the same time. The signs fulfill expectations and disappoint them. But the reason for this is that the Lord to whom they point is himself uncapturable, by either his friends or his foes.

15

Three Surprises

We find in one simple chapter of Matthew's Gospel—chapter 13—six parables. Of these six, three stand in a special connection to each other. Their special literary form places them into a unit in that the first parable—the Wheat and the Weeds—is followed by two very short parables—the Mustard Seed, and the Leaven. Then, following the second and third parables, the first one is explained by Jesus. Since, according to Matthew's account, Jesus told them together, I want to consider them together.

Another parable he put before them, saying, "The kingdom of heaven may be compared to a man who sowed good seed in his field; but while men were sleeping, his enemy came and sowed weeds among the wheat, and went away. So when the plants came up and bore grain, then the weeds appeared also.

And the servants of the householder came and said to him, 'Sir, did you not sow good seed in your field? How then has it weeds?' He said to them, 'An enemy has done this.' The servants said to him, 'Then do you want us to go and gather them?' But he said, 'No; lest in gathering the weeds you root up the wheat along with them. Let both grow together until the harvest; and at harvest time I will tell the reapers, Gather the weeds first and bind them in bundles to be burned, but gather the wheat into my barn.'"

—*Matt. 13:24–30*

This short story tells of the planting of wheat by a farmer. An enemy then plants weeds in the same field. When the workers discover and report the disaster of this treachery, they expect instructions from the owner to uproot the weeds. The surprise of the story comes at this point. The owner tells them to allow the weeds to grow with the wheat until the harvest, at which time a judging can then occur, with the wheat gathered into the barns and the weeds thrown into the fire. Later, in verses 37–43, when Jesus interprets this parable to his disciples, he identifies the wheat as the children of the kingdom and the weeds as the sons of the evil one. Jesus does not explain what he means by the description "sons of the evil one," whereas from other New Testament texts we understand that the sons of the kingdom are those who have faith in Jesus Christ (John 1:1–18).

What does Jesus intend therefore by the phrase: "sons of the evil one"? Later in the paragraph he tells of the judgment in which the angels "will gather out of his kingdom all causes of sin and all evildoers . . ." (v. 41). Does Jesus intend the phrase to refer to all the activities and powers of the devil such as demons, temptation, and evil itself, as well as "all evildoers"? This broader description makes the most sense in the light of the total context of this passage.

This parable communicates with tremendous hitting force because we who hear it are very aware of the terrible weeds that harass humankind: war, temptation to evil, terrorism in the name of just causes, despair and hopelessness brought on by human injustice, and every other pressure toward dehumanization.

The Sons of the Kingdom

The parable tells of the existence of the planted wheat of the sons of the kingdom. It also tells of the stark reality of the existence of the weeds which have their origin in moral, personal evil, which is the devil, the twisted one ("evil" is the word *ponēros* which means "twist"). The parable tells that the wheat must somehow manage to grow to maturity alongside the weeds. Finally, it promises that in the final harvest there will be a weighing and a division so that evil and its rank growth will be destroyed while the sons of the kingdom will be honored at that great harvest.

The surprise in this parable, as we have observed, is centered upon the decision of the lord of the field to refuse the workers' request to destroy the weeds. This means that Jesus has rejected our request for special and favorable growing conditions for the wheat. Somehow and in some way the wheat must survive and grow to maturity (harvest time) in a less than ideal setting, just as we must build houses that are able to withstand wind and rain (Matt. 7).

Because of this refusal on Jesus' part we find ourselves resisting the logic of this parable. Most of us spend a lot of time and money in various attempts to ensure that our children grow up in ideal settings wherever that is possible. We select schools and neighborhoods with this in mind. We have read the Parable of the Soils and therefore we try hard to arrange for a place for our Christian lives and the lives of our families to grow that is not cluttered with thorns and other competitors for the growth of genuine faith.

A Profound Contest All of the Way

Now, in this parable which is told by Jesus immediately following the Parable of the Soils, our Lord teaches that all growth toward maturity must take place amidst weeds that are very close to our lives. We are to journey alongside the competitors of faith, hope, and love. And the journey is to be a profound contest all of the way to the moment of final evaluation by God himself. The parable is realistic, though, at first glance, the realistic portrayal is hardly encouraging. But the more we reflect upon the very elements in the parable that are disappointing to our expectations, the more we make marvelous breakthrough discoveries.

First, this parable in its very realism assures us that Jesus is fully aware of the true growing conditions in which we must somehow make it! Jesus has not idealized the Christian life or the Christian church with a portrait of endless victories and joys. Instead, we have the portrait of parents who ask for the ideal place to raise their young and the word comes back to them—"No, raise your sons and daughters right where they are and know that I know where they are. I know the field, I know of the weeds, and I know of your concerns." The profound note of hope in the parable is just this knowing which Jesus has shown us by his story about wheat and weeds.

The second exciting discovery we make in this parable is that the strategy of Jesus Christ in the world is intentionally and deliberately *person oriented*. Human beings are the generic reality in this parable and they are the harvest of hope that Jesus the great Farmer has in mind.

We now know that there can be no solution of the crisis of history that does not grapple with man and woman, because both the hope and the crisis are related to the human part of the equation.

The large question on everyone's mind is this—what are the prospects in all of this? The answer from Jesus is both realistic and hopeful at the same time. There is a contest going on for growing space and there is no escaping that contest, but the harvest is assured by the storyteller. In that harvest the wheat will be there to be counted and celebrated. The next two parables in this trilogy help us to understand why Jesus is so sure of that harvest.

Another parable he put before them, saying, "The kingdom of heaven is like a grain of mustard seed which a man took and sowed in his field; it is the smallest of all seeds, but when it has grown it is the greatest of shrubs and becomes a tree, so that the birds of the air come and make nests in its branches."
—*Matt. 13:31, 32*

This brief parable about a mustard seed follows the more complex wheat and weeds parable, a parable that is crisscrossed with discouraging elements and the stark realization of the kind of world in which we must live our lives. Now, in this very simple story, we hear about the tiny mustard seed that grows to a height of ten to twelve feet, a tree that birds favor because they eat its tiny seeds. Jesus tells his hearers that the kingdom of God is like that tiny mustard seed and its great bush.

The Meaning of the Mustard Seed

What does he mean to teach with this one-sentence parable? The kingly reign of Christ is small at the beginning and yet it grows to a surprising size. The question that the parable requires us to ask is this: In what sense is Christ's reign ever small? If we can understand this theme that stands at the very core of the Messiahship of Jesus Christ as it is both disclosed and hidden throughout our Lord's ministry, then we will be able to come very close to the theological heartbeat of the gospel. This is a parable about the power of Jesus Christ. It reminds us of the smallness of God's mighty act in the coming of Jesus Christ. We know from the intertestamental expectations that stirred within the Jewish nation that by the time of the first century the hopes for Messiah were bold and militant. Second Esdras tells of the raising of the Lion of Judah, John the Baptist tells of the Messiah who will hold the great blade in his hand to clear the threshing floor.

But what happens when, in fact, the Messiah does come? Jesus arrives as an infant without either a palace or a revolutionary encampment to protect him and his destiny. Jesus, in his ministry, is a disappointment to John the Baptist and it is the smallness of his style and ministry that stands out most clearly for any reader of the Gospels. This parable is a hidden parable about the humiliation of the smallness of Christ, a smallness that is overwhelmed by the rush of politics and treachery on the day we now call Good Friday. Jesus is indeed very small because his way of conquering evil demands that he must take its full weight upon himself. Jesus does not conquer Pilate or Caiaphas. He conquers the weapons they use, but to do that he must disarm these weapons of death. And that disarming is done through death and by the victory of resurrection. This parable tells of the power of life which grows from utter smallness toward the substantial shrub that birds respect and desire.

Secondly, this parable also refers to the kingdom strategy of Jesus in the world. His strategy begins with the small and moves by single steps toward meaningful size. Jesus begins with the smallness of a few disciples who are entrusted with the good news of Christ's redeeming Lordship. These disciples have a very large and vast truth to tell, but they themselves are quite small and insignificant in the scale of political power in the first-century world. But there is a promise that is fundamental to the parable, and that promise is hidden in the mystery of God's power at work in the small beginnings of his kingdom. The secret is his power and life hidden in the small single step.

What are the implications of this brief but important parable for us, as people of the kingly reign of Christ in today's world? I believe that the parable challenges us not to abandon the smallness of the gospel in favor of the sizes that tempt us. The parable tells us that we should have confidence in Jesus Christ himself. He is all that we need and we must understand that any addition of power that we seek to add to Christ himself is in reality a subtraction from our confidence in the all-sufficiency of Christ. The parable encourages us to celebrate the wondrous smallness of the Christ who emptied himself and took upon himself the form of a slave (Phil. 2). He is all that we need, and the miracle of the gospel is that God's mighty Son is the servant who became small in our favor. This holy smallness grows toward a mighty fulfillment of hope and fruitfulness. But Jesus has yet one more parable to tell about hiddenness.

> He told them another parable. "The kingdom of heaven is like leaven which a woman took and hid in three measures of flour, till it was all leavened."
> —*Matt. 13:33*

Leaven is the yeast used to transform flour and water into bread. The leaven is hidden in the flour and though it cannot be seen it totally alters the moist flour into the dough ready for baking.

Some interpreters of this parable have concluded that the leaven here refers to the corruption of the church that grows in a hidden way within the church. These interpreters (i.e., Teelman) see this parable as a prophecy by Jesus of heresies and corruptions that would assault the church. They have come to this conclusion because they argue that leaven is always used in Scripture as a symbol of evil (1 Cor. 5:7, Luke 12:1, Gal. 5:9). In the Old Testament Law (Exod. 13:3; Lev. 2:11), the children of Israel are commanded to carefully put leaven out of their houses during Passover week, and not to use it in certain sacrifices. This was to be a sign of the purging of sin and malice out of their lives.

However, I do not believe that our Lord has told this parable with that in mind. This use of yeast as an image is about the kingdom of heaven and its context is not negative, but powerfully positive. Richard Trench gives us wise counsel in regard to the interpretive challenge of this parable: "We ought not, then, to take the parable in other than its obvious sense, that it prophesies the diffusion, and not the corruption of the gospel. By the leaven we are to understand the Word of the Kingdom; which word, in its highest sense, Christ himself was."[1] Trench's rule for interpretation is always the best rule. We should interpret every text in "its obvious sense" before we seek any specialized or imposed interpretation. We know that Jesus has demonstrated in his parables a method of storytelling that surprises our expectations. The laborers parable has shocked expectations, so also has the Parable of the Unjust Steward. Therefore we should not be surprised that his household-cooking parable tells of leaven in a nonreligious and common-sense manner. We are tampering with the parable when we impose upon Jesus' parable about

1. Richard Trench, *Notes on the Parables of Our Lord* (Grand Rapids, Mich.: Baker, 1970), 119.

hiddenness any meaning that is not warranted within the text itself.

A Parable of Patience

This is a brief story about the hiddenness of the kingly reign of Christ. The word of that kingdom is not only small like the mustard seed; it is almost invisible to the eyes of those who don't know how to look for it. The key theme in this parable is that the kingdom power of God may be hidden for a while, but given time, its lively effect will be known for all to see and even taste! If I trust in this parable of Jesus, I will be willing to trust in the eventual vindication of the reign of the King even though here and now it does not seem that this apparently nonvisible leaven of God's word is having any effect at all. The parable teaches that we who are God's people must be willing to wait for the good effect of what God is doing in people's lives, because a journey is involved that takes time. We must be willing to take the time required. In my own journey as a Christian I have learned that this parable of patience is one of the most vital ones to learn for those who are highly "action-" and "results-oriented." It is not a truth that I welcome at first glance because I would prefer a more visible and publicly dynamic strategy.

Jesus shows his authority in these three parables, and he also shows his patience. It is a patience that has its origins in confidence in the durable power of truth. Therefore each of these hidden parables is a parable about hope—but hope that takes its time.

16

Asking the Impossible

Jesus not only told the people parables. He also did things that were to have an illustrative and parabolic effect. One of the most dramatic of these is the incident that occurred at the beginning of our Lord's entry into the city of Jerusalem on Palm Sunday. Mark's Gospel tells us of this incident.

On the following day, when they came from Bethany, he was hungry. And seeing in the distance a fig tree in leaf, he went to see if he could find anything on it. When he came to it, he found nothing but leaves, for it was not the season for figs. And he said to it, "May no one ever eat fruit from you again." And his disciples heard it. . . . As they passed by in the morning, they saw the fig tree withered away to its roots. And Peter remembered and said to him, "Master, look! The fig tree which you cursed has withered." And Jesus answered them, "Have faith in God. Truly, I say to you, whoever says to this mountain, 'Be taken up and cast into the sea,' and does not doubt in his heart, but believes that what he says will come to pass, it will be done for him. Therefore I tell you, whatever you ask in prayer, believe that you receive it, and you will. And whenever you stand praying, forgive, if you have anything against any one; so that your Father also who is in heaven may forgive you your trespasses."

—Mark 11:12–14, 20–26

This is not a spoken parable; it is an event that happened right in front of the disciples' eyes, an event with parabolic effect. It is an acted-out parable.

In this incident Jesus looks for figs from the fig tree and he finds none; Mark comes to the defense of the fig tree, "for it was not the season for figs." Nevertheless Jesus speaks the words of rebuke: "'May no one ever eat fruit from you again.'" The next day the disciples notice that the tree is now withered to its roots, and Peter tells Jesus of this amazing fact. At this point the surprise occurs in this living-event parable.

An Analogy from a Fig Tree

We would expect Jesus to point up some possible analogy between the judgment fate of the fig tree and the judgment that awaits fruitlessness in our lives—an analogy between fruitless leafy fig trees and fruitless leafy human lives. But instead of this expected discourse on judgment, Jesus gives his disciples words of hope and tells them of the incredible power in prayer for those who ask in faith. He also teaches his disciples about forgiveness and the importance he has placed upon our need to forgive other people who have wronged us. This is not a discourse on judgment but of prayer and of forgiveness.

This surprise conclusion to the fig-tree incident forces the reader of this Gospel to wonder about its actual meaning. If it baffled Peter and the disciples when they experienced the event, it also baffles disciples today.

From an interpretive standpoint the most helpful approach to such a passage is first to ask plainly what is happening in the story line. One possibility in this event is that Jesus asks for early figs from this leafy tree and when none are found he rightly judges the tree because of its barrenness. This is the approach to interpretation that most New Testament commentators have taken. The rebuke of barrenness does make sense. Humanity, made in the image of God, with all of its advantages of freedom and authority, has been able to put forth very little real fruit; and the events of Holy Week will point to that bankruptcy of spiritual and moral fruitfulness. Religion with all of its leaves will fail during this awesome week, as will the secular power of Roman civilization. Even Jesus' disciples themselves will fail to meet the obligations placed upon their lives. They too will prove fruitless in spite of the advantages they had and in spite of all they had experienced through their journeys with Jesus Christ.

I think the deeper interpretive clue to this incident grows out of Mark's statement in defense of the tree: "It was not the season for figs." I do not think that Jesus is here granting a dramatic sign in order to warn the disciples against the lack of fruitfulness. I think the purpose is deeper and more basic than that scolding bit of obvious advice. Jesus asks of the tree what is not in its nature to supply. By his defensive statement concerning the season, Mark has ruled out that we should expect figs, even the early figs (taksh) that appear at the opening of the growing season. Jesus has asked of the tree what it cannot supply. And when that essential inability is revealed, Jesus speaks a word of judgment that does not immediately take effect. Instead, the next day they all realize the terrible finality of the judgment word spoken by Jesus.

The Most Important Fruit Jesus Seeks

What can this event mean theologically for the disciples, and for us? What is clear is one thing—Jesus asks of us what we cannot hope to supply from within the essential nature of who we are. He asks in the spring season for figs that we cannot offer to him. The most important fruit Jesus now requests of every man or woman is a fruit we cannot of ourselves be expected to supply. What is that impossible fruit? Certainly, Jesus intends the powerful gifts for which we must pray when we cry to God for help, and chief among these is the forgiveness of sins. We cannot confer forgiveness upon ourselves except in the distorted religious world of "cheap grace." What we need most for life and living we cannot find within ourselves, and it never is found in a springtime fig tree. But it must be found in God. This is therefore an acted-out parable that surprises us with the wonder of God's grace as the only true source of that most essential of all fruitfulness. The fig tree incident is similar in its theme to the parable Jesus told (John 15) of himself as the True Vine, and of us as the branches. His warning in that parable picks up this theme, "without me you can do nothing."

There are other event-parables in the life and ministry of Jesus. Joachim Jeremias sees the moment that Jesus wrote in the sand (John 8) as one such scene-parable in which Jesus does something unforgettable while at the same time, mysterious and hidden. A crowd is screaming its rage at a rejected woman caught in adultery. Jesus stands alongside this woman and he tells the tempters who have used her life to entrap him that the one without guilt should throw the first stone. Then he stoops to write in the sand; he does not move to safety away from the one who may be momentarily stoned by the crowd. All of humanity can never forget this sand-writing moment when Jesus slowed down a furious crowd and saved them from doing more harm than they had already done in tempting the Son of God. He also rescued the life of a woman; perhaps she was Mary Magdalene. We cannot forget the sand and yet we know nothing more than that he wrote in the sand. This is a totally hidden Messianic event-parable. It actually happened as an event and its significance is profound though we can hardly capture it in words.

On the Thursday evening of Holy Week our Lord presented to his disciples his most important parable-event of his ministry; it happened during their celebration of the Seder meal. Jesus took the cup of thanksgiving and gave to that cup a sign value beyond its ancient Exodus significance. It became in its pouring out the sign of his life poured out. He took bread, and in breaking the bread Jesus called that breaking a sign of his life broken in favor of all men and women, so that by receiving the sign of the cup and broken bread the disciples were celebrating the sign of Christ's sacrificial presence until he would come again. This final mysterious note of victory and ultimate triumph puts this sign of the Lord's Supper on an eternal stage and landscape of God's design.

Why did Jesus entrust his teaching on the vital themes of the gospel to parables which by their very nature can be misunderstood? Why would Jesus judge the fig tree, write in sand, offer wine and broken bread to his disciples, and wash their feet as a sign of holy servanthood?

Jesus is so sure of himself and the content of his ministry and message that he takes the risk of parables. Jesus entrusts these stories we call parables into our hearts and minds so that they become ours to treasure and to love. But more than that, they become teachers that point our eyes to Christ himself. We learn from the parables how good he is, how he surprises our expectation, how he calls to us to follow him as his disciples.

The parables finally belong to their teacher and they cannot go beyond the teacher himself. He is their main subject and because of this they never grow old. There is a playful, even whimsical, youthfulness about all of the parables which, I believe, is why children love to hear them told. We must never forget this playfulness in the stories Jesus told because when we reach the fulfillment of all life, called heaven, we will hear laughter there. The laughter of joy—"We sin and grow old but our Father is younger than we" (G. K. Chesterton). Perhaps the laughter in heaven will be one of the best of all gifts we experience there. And the parables of Jesus have invited us to begin experiencing it right now.

Bibliography

Albright, William F., and Mann, C. S. *Matthew,* The Anchor Bible, vol. 26. New York: Doubleday, 1971.

Baly, Denis. *Basic Biblical Geography.* Philadelphia: Fortress, 1987.

Bornkamm, Gunther. *Jesus of Nazareth.* New York: Harper and Row, 1975.

Bruce, F. F. *New Testament History.* New York: Doubleday, 1972.

Bruner, F. Dale. *The Christbook.* Waco, Tex.: Word, 1987.

Dodd, C. H. *The Bible and the Greeks.* London: Hodder and Stoughton, 1964.

———. *The Parables of the Kingdom,* rev. ed. New York: Scribners, 1961.

Geldenhuys, J. N. *Commentary on Luke,* New International Commentary on the New Testament. Grand Rapids: Eerdmans, 1951.

Hunter, A. M. *The Gospel According to John,* Cambridge Bible Commentary on the New English Bible. Cambridge: Cambridge University Press, 1976.

Jeremias, Joachim. *Jerusalem in the Time of Jesus.* Philadelphia: Fortress, 1969.

———. *New Testament Theology.* New York: Scribners, 1971.

———. *Rediscovering the Parables.* New York: Scribners, 1966.

Trench, R. C. *Notes on the Parables of Our Lord.* Westwood, N.J.: Revell, 1953.

Study Guide
Questions for Reflection

For use in personal or group Bible study.

1. **Jesus the Teacher**
   a. Mark describes Jesus as a teacher. What are the different ways that Jesus teaches his disciples in this chapter?
   b. Why does Jesus tell parables? What reasons does he give? What are your own feelings? What do you feel are the advantages and weaknesses in parables as a way of teaching?
   c. In-depth question: Draw up your own descriptive list of the kinds of teaching that you notice from the New Testament records of Jesus.

2. **Laughter in Heaven** (Luke 15)
   a. How would you describe the kinds of lostness that Jesus portrays in the three parables?
   b. How do the three parables portray the character of God?
   c. In-depth question: How do the parables of Jesus teach about his own character? Draw up your own list with your notations of the kinds of portrayals you find.

3. **Four Debtors** (Matt. 18:23–35; Luke 7:40–50)
   a. In what way is forgiveness a powerful experience? How does Jesus define the experience of forgiveness and its meaning in these parables?
   b. What do you feel is the significance of these parables

for today? Are they needed for our generation? In
what ways?

4. **The Existence of God**   (Luke 16:19–31)
   a. What do you think this parable teaches about the
      dynamics of believing?
   b. Why do you feel the proofs for God are declined by
      Abraham in the story?

5. **A Question of Time**   (Matt. 13:3–8)
   a. Can you think of twentieth-century connections to
      this parable's portrayal of the soils?
   b. If this parable were described to you as a "freedom
      parable," what do you feel that means?

6. **To Finally Believe**   (Matt. 21:28–32)
   a. What insights into the meaning of faith do you gain
      from this parable?
   b. What did you learn about the will of God for human
      life from this parable?
   c. In-depth question: Draw up your own list of parables
      that teach the meaning of prayer; note the different
      emphasis in each.

7. **The Good Shepherd**   (John 10:1–30)
   a. What do you learn about Jesus Christ in this parable
      as he describes himself?
   b. What do you learn about the obligations and the re-
      wards of discipleship from this parable?
   c. In-depth question: Trace the great "I Am" sentences
      of this Gospel. In what ways are they parabolically
      exciting? What is the main emphasis of each?

8. **The Foundation That Lasts**   (Matt. 7:24–29)
   a. We are described as house-builders by Jesus. In what
      ways is this a helpful description? In what ways do I
      find that description challenging?
   b. Jesus Christ's words and deeds are described as the
      solid foundation. How do I make Christ the foundation

of my life? Are there steps to be followed? Is it a once-and-for-all moment or a journey experience?

9. **The Friends of the King**   (Matt. 20:1–16)
   a. Why do you feel that Jesus ignores such a commonly held value as the payment-for-work expectations represented in this parable?
   b. In what ways is the generosity of the lord of the estate shown?
   c. In-depth question: Trace in your journal other examples in which Jesus challenges and surprises the values that are commonly held. Explain your cited examples.

10. **One Road at a Time**   (Luke 10:25–37)
    a. How does Jesus teach ethics in this parable? Describe his approach.
    b. What are some of the surprises you found in this parable?

11. **A Matter of Importance**   (Luke 19:11–27; 16:1–13)
    a. What role does fear play in this parable?
    b. What is the role that freedom plays in these parables?
    c. In-depth question: Draw together your own collection of stewardship parables.

12. **Prayer**   (Luke 18:1–14)
    a. Why do you feel these two parables are told together? How do the stories compliment each other?
    b. From the two parables, what do you learn about prayer from Christ?

13. **Invitation to a Banquet**   (Matt. 22:1–14; Luke 14:15–24)
    a. Why is the host angry at his intended guests?
    b. How did you respond at a feeling level toward these parables?
    c. In-depth question: Notice how invitations to celebration play a key role in other parables. Trace these other settings and draw together your own reflections

on the significance of these celebrations in Jesus'
teaching.

14. **The Hidden Parables**   (John 2:13–22)
    a. Why do you think Jesus told parables that are hard to
       understand?
    b. In what ways do these parables help to put together a
       total portrait of Jesus?

15. **Three Surprises**   (Matt. 13:24–33)
    a. What are the elements in these three parables that
       take your own expectations by surprise?
    b. In what way is Jesus Christ himself like the mustard
       seed and the leaven?

16. **Asking the Impossible**   (Mark 11:12–14, 20–26)
    a. Why do you feel Christ creates a crisis like the fig-
       tree incident for his disciples?
    b. What is the message of hope in the fig-tree incident?

LaVergne, TN USA
28 December 2009
168090LV00002B/50/A